Computers for Seniors

COMPUTERS FOR SENIORS

EMAIL, INTERNET, PHOTOS, AND MORE IN 14 EASY LESSONS

CHRIS EWIN, CARRIE EWIN, AND CHERYL EWIN

no starch
press

SAN FRANCISCO

Printed in USA
First printing

21 20 19 18 17   1 2 3 4 5 6 7 8 9

ISBN-10: 1-59327-792-X
ISBN-13: 978-1-59327-792-5

Publisher: William Pollock
Production Editor: Serena Yang
Cover Design: Beth Middleworth
Interior Design: Serena Yang
Developmental Editor: Liz Chadwick
Copyeditor: Barton D. Reed
Compositor: Serena Yang
Proofreader: Emelie Burnette

Photo of desktop computer on page 3 by Denis Rozhnovsky/Shutterstock.com. Photo of laptop computer on page 3 by ifong/Shutterstock.com. Photo on page 4 by Roman Samokhin/Shutterstock.com. Photo on page 8 by PJjaruwan/Shutterstock.com. Photo on page 10 by Jason Stitt/Shutterstock.com. Photo of laptop computer on page 13 by Suwan Waenlor/Shutterstock.com. Photo of tablet on page 13 by time4studio/Shutterstock.com. Photo of mouse on page 14 by yanugkelid/Shutterstock.com. Photo of touchpad on page 14 by imagedb.com/ Shutterstock.com. Diagram of keyboard on page 16 by Igor Kyrlytsya/Shutterstock.com. Photo of USB cable on page 294 by Lifestyle_Studio/Shutterstock.com.

For information on distribution, translations, or bulk sales, please contact No Starch Press, Inc. directly:

No Starch Press, Inc.
245 8th Street, San Francisco, CA 94103
phone: 1.415.863.9900; info@nostarch.com; www.nostarch.com

Cataloging-in-Publication Data is available from the Library of Congress.

Brief Contents

Contents in Detail

Acknowledgments

What a journey! There are so many people to thank for making this book possible. We'd like to thank Rojer Liberman for founding the Chelsea PC Support Group, which started us off on our teaching journey so many years ago. Our thanks also to Alex Taylor and Leslie Trevena for all of their support. Our sincerest thanks as well to Lorna Stevenson for being a wonderful rock of support.

We'd also like to thank all the wonderful people at No Starch Press. From making excellent improvements, to incorporating our many changes (because one of us is a perfectionist!), to making things look amazing, there's nothing you haven't been ready to do. Most especially, our passionate thanks to Bill Pollock, Liz Chadwick, and Serena Yang.

Our thanks also to all of the clients of Enhance Computer Services. In particular, thanks to Arnold Luby and the other clients who have been with us since the beginning. We've been thrilled by your support and encouragement.

Of course, not a step of this journey would have been possible without the endless number of delightful seniors we've had the pleasure of teaching over the years at Seniors IT and the Chelsea PC Support Group. Thank you all, particularly those who took the time to give us feedback and ideas!

INTRODUCTION

Welcome to *Computers for Seniors*! Your computer is a hub for entertainment, communication, and getting work done. This book will help you use your computer to its full potential, taking you from zero knowledge to being comfortable finding your way around. You'll learn how to keep in touch with friends and family as well as enjoy free music, videos, and books. You'll also learn how to explore the internet, use practical and entertaining apps, and protect yourself from viruses and other threats.

You'll learn about your computer's most useful features in a simple and straightforward way. We'll cover many new features introduced in Windows 10, so whether you're starting out with your first computer or just want to learn about the newest features available, this is the book for you!

About This Book

This book was inspired by our experience working with seniors. We've been teaching computer skills to seniors for a combined 30 years and have created our own Seniors IT program dedicated to helping seniors learn how to use computers in a simple way and with easy activities. Over the years, we've been asked many times to turn our famous Seniors IT classes into a book so people can learn when and where they want. Well, here we are!

Computers for Seniors will teach you to use your computer in the same lesson-by-lesson format we teach to seniors in our classrooms. That means we'll cover only the truly useful features that other seniors have requested, used, and loved. This book provides step-by-step instructions and full-color pictures to make things as easy to follow as possible. No dry reading here! We hope this book will help you learn the things you truly want to know about your computer.

Who Should Read This Book?

This book is perfect for all seniors, wherever you fall within that age range, who want to use the computer to stay in touch with people via email or calls, play games, manage photos, explore the internet, or just have fun. We start from scratch, so even if you've never used a mouse or keyboard before, you'll be able to follow along in this book. If you have a little more experience, you're well catered to with our "Explore" sections, which will help guide you to adventure through bigger ideas and products. You'll also enjoy discovering lots of new Windows 10 features for work and play.

What You'll Need

You'll need a computer device with Windows 10 and an internet connection. Your computer might be a desktop computer, a laptop, or a tablet of any brand—and any version of Windows 10 will work perfectly fine! If you're upgrading to Windows 10 from an older version, like Windows 7 or Windows 8, this book is also for you.

If you don't have a computer yet, fear not! We'll begin with a guide to the sort of computer to buy, how to set up Windows 10, and how to connect to the internet.

Some of the topics covered in this book also require a webcam and speakers. A laptop or tablet computer will have these built in, but if you have a desktop, you might need to buy them separately.

How to Read This Book

We strongly recommend you read this book in order, because every lesson builds on the previous one. For example, you'll need to learn to put photos on your computer before you learn to send photos via email!

Every lesson includes activities that put your learning into practice, so you should aim to complete those activities. There are solutions at the back of the book if you get stuck or would like some guidance (see "Solutions" on page 305). A couple of lessons and activities will ask you to work with a friend or family member to do things like making and receiving Skype calls. If you can't find anyone to help you at that moment, feel free to leave the activity and come back to it later.

The "Explore" sections are designed to encourage you to go further on your own and explore features, apps, and websites that might interest you. "Explore" sections provide help and guidance but not step-by-step instructions. Feel free to try out the "Explore" sections that interest you, but they are in no way mandatory.

What's in This Book?

You'll begin by learning about the different types of computers and devices and then get tips for what to look for when buying one. Then you'll learn how set up your computer out of the box and how to use the keyboard and mouse. Once you're set up, you'll be ready for the lessons:

* **Lesson 1: Getting Started** shows you how to navigate the first things you'll see when you turn your computer on, and how to open and close an app.

* **Lesson 2: Introducing Apps** familiarizes you with some of the useful apps included on your computer, such as the Calendar app, the Weather app, and the Solitaire game.

* **Lesson 3: The Photos App** shows you how to transfer photos from your phone or camera onto your computer and view them whenever you like.

* **Lesson 4: Email** shows you how to send, receive, and reply to emails and how to send attachments such as photos.

* **Lesson 5: Introducing the Internet** teaches you how to use the internet to browse websites.

* **Lesson 6: Exploring the Internet** shows you how to search for things on the internet and introduces some wonderful websites to try out.

* **Lesson 7: Watching TV and Videos Online** helps you find instructional and entertaining videos to watch on your computer.

* **Lesson 8: Downloading New Apps** shows you how to find useful and entertaining apps such as games, language translators, and more.

* **Lesson 9: Listening to Music Online** shows you how to listen to your favorite music for free on the internet.

* **Lesson 10: Reading Ebooks with OverDrive** shows you how to borrow and read books on your computer for free.

* **Lesson 11: Making Calls with Skype** shows you how to make audio and video calls with friends and family via Skype.

* **Lesson 12: Typing Letters and Documents** shows you how to use WordPad to create professional-looking documents (such as letters) on your computer.

* **Lesson 13: Files and Folders** helps you organize your computer so that you can easily find your pictures and documents.

* **Lesson 14: Staying Safe Online** teaches you the things you need to know to stay safe and protect yourself against viruses and scams.

At the end of the book are a few short reference guides to help you connect extra devices to your computer, create a Microsoft account, and connect to free Wi-Fi networks outside your home. By the time you finish this book, you'll be confident using the most enjoyable and useful parts of your computer.

What Else Do You Need to Know?

Although every effort has been made to make sure this book is as up-to-date as possible, Windows 10 is constantly improving, and you might find that small details have changed between the time this book was printed and when it reached your hands. For example, the screenshots might look slightly different from what you see onscreen, or a button might have a different name or color. Regardless, you should still be able to identify what you need from the images provided.

Let's get started!

BUYING AND SETTING UP YOUR COMPUTER

In this lesson, you'll learn about the different types of computers, what to look for when purchasing a computer, and how to set up your new computer.

In the 14 easy lessons in this book, you'll learn to do useful, entertaining, and exciting things with your computer, such as how to write and send emails; organize photos; keep in touch with loved ones; and find books, movies, music, and more on the internet.

But before you can take advantage of all that a computer has to offer, you need to choose a computer and learn how to set it up. In the following pages, we'll show you the different types of computers and offer advice to help you choose the one that's right for you. We'll also demonstrate how to connect and set up your new computer.

If you already have a computer set up and you're comfortable using the keyboard and mouse, you can skip forward to Lesson 1.

Choosing a Computer

The first step of your journey begins with choosing a computer. When you're shopping for a computer, it's important to know what kind will suit your needs so you can get one that works best for you.

WHAT KIND OF COMPUTER DO I NEED?

Computers come in all different shapes and sizes! The largest type of computer is a *desktop*, which sits on or under your desk and isn't portable. The smallest computer you'll find is a *tablet*, which you can carry around with you everywhere. A *laptop* is somewhere in between. Deciding between a desktop, a laptop, and a tablet is the first important choice to make when buying a new computer. Let's take a look at each of these.

Desktops

A desktop computer is designed to sit on or under your desk. It usually consists of a *tower*, which does all the actual work of the computer, and a *monitor*, which is the screen you look at. Desktops have large screens, which is great if you need items on the screen to look bigger.

Desktop computers are heavy and need to be plugged into a power outlet, so they usually just stay at a desk in your home and aren't intended to be portable. This means you won't be able to take your desktop with you on vacation! They also take up more space than other types of computers, which can be a downside if you live in a small apartment.

Laptops

Laptops are smaller, lightweight computers that can comfortably fit on your lap, which is wonderful if you like the idea of using your computer while lounging in your favorite chair. Most laptops weigh only a few pounds, so you can easily move them from room to room, work on them at the dining table or in front of the TV, or even take them with you on vacation. The battery should last for a few hours while the laptop is not plugged in, so you can use it on the go.

The trade-offs for this more portable, convenient computer are that the screen is smaller than that of a desktop, and a laptop is often a little less powerful than a desktop of the same price. We'll look at what makes a computer powerful a little later.

Tablets

These small computers are the most portable you'll find. In fact, the entire computer is built into the small screen. They're great for carrying around with you and are easy to use on the train, on vacation, or at a coffee shop. Tablets don't come with a keyboard, so you'll need to tap the screen to type anything. This can be a bit awkward, so many tablet users buy separate keyboards, but they're clunky and detract from the portability a bit. Tablets also have much smaller screens and relatively little space for storing photos, music, and other files. They tend to be more expensive than desktops or laptops of comparable power or storage space.

> **✱ NOTE:** This book covers only Windows tablets. There are other types of tablets, such as Apple iPads and Android tablets, but they work quite differently.

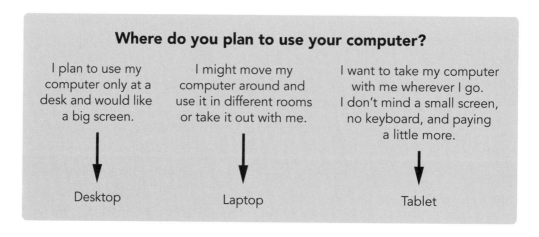

Where do you plan to use your computer?

I plan to use my computer only at a desk and would like a big screen.	I might move my computer around and use it in different rooms or take it out with me.	I want to take my computer with me wherever I go. I don't mind a small screen, no keyboard, and paying a little more.
↓	↓	↓
Desktop	Laptop	Tablet

WHAT SPECIFICATIONS DO I NEED?

Once you've decided on the type of computer you want, you'll need to choose a specific model. With so many different models available, picking the right one for you can feel daunting. But don't worry! This section gives you the information you need to choose the perfect computer for you.

Many companies use technical terms to advertise their products. These terms describe some of the most important parts of a computer, so it's useful to know what they mean. Let's go over some of these terms to help you decide what you want in your new computer, and then we'll pose a few questions to help you decide which computer is right for you.

Processor

The *processor* is like the brain of the computer. The better your processor, the faster and more responsive your computer will be. When we say a computer is powerful, we're saying that it has a lot of *processing power*. Some common processors are the Intel Pentium, Core i3, Core i5, and Core i7. An Intel Pentium or Core i3 will be fine for most computer tasks, like sending emails and browsing the internet, but a Core i5 or Core i7 will perform better, making your computer run faster and feel more responsive. If you're unsure, a Core i3 or Core i5 is usually a safe bet!

RAM

RAM, which stands for *random access memory*, is the computer's short-term memory. Everything you do on your computer uses a little piece of RAM. Just like a person trying to remember lots of different numbers, names, and tasks at the same time, your computer can become slow if it's trying to juggle too many tasks at once—the more RAM it has, the more tasks it can do simultaneously.

RAM is measured in *gigabytes (GB)*. Computers need at least 4 gigabytes (4GB) of RAM; 8 gigabytes (8GB) is even better, but not essential unless you plan to do more demanding tasks such as video editing or want to have lots of different things open on your computer at one time.

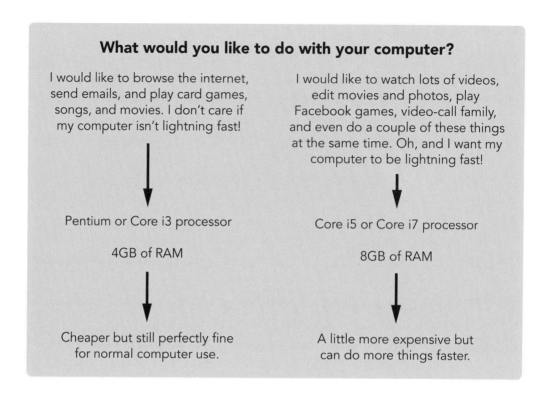

What would you like to do with your computer?

I would like to browse the internet, send emails, and play card games, songs, and movies. I don't care if my computer isn't lightning fast!

I would like to watch lots of videos, edit movies and photos, play Facebook games, video-call family, and even do a couple of these things at the same time. Oh, and I want my computer to be lightning fast!

Pentium or Core i3 processor

4GB of RAM

Core i5 or Core i7 processor

8GB of RAM

Cheaper but still perfectly fine for normal computer use.

A little more expensive but can do more things faster.

Hard Drive

The hard drive is the computer's long-term memory. Everything you save on your computer to use again, including letters, photos, videos, songs, and programs, is stored on the hard drive. The bigger the hard drive, the more you can store on your computer! Like RAM, hard drives are also measured in gigabytes. However, because hard drives can be a lot larger than RAM, you might also see them advertised in *terabytes (TB)*, where 1 terabyte is equal to 1000 gigabytes.

If you don't plan to store lots of photos, music, or videos, then a hard drive that's 60GB or larger will be perfectly fine. If you're a movie or music buff and plan to keep a collection on your computer, look for a hard drive with at least 500GB. Generally, 1GB of hard drive space stores around an hour of home video or around 200 photos or songs, but remember that you'll also need room for your apps, emails, and Windows itself! You can expect these to use up at least 40GB of your hard drive.

* **150GB Hard Drive:** Up to 150 hours of home videos, 40 movies, 30,000 photos, or 40,000 songs.

* **500GB Hard Drive:** Up to 500 hours of home videos, 120 movies, 100,000 photos, or 125,000 songs.

* **300GB Hard Drive:** Up to 300 hours of home videos, 80 movies, 60,000 photos, or 80,000 songs.

DVD Drive

A DVD drive lets you insert and play both music CDs and video DVDs. Almost all desktops and many laptops come with a DVD drive, but tablets don't. The one downside about a DVD drive in a laptop is that it makes the laptop heavier and thicker, so it's more difficult to take it around with you. Nonetheless, if you think you're likely to need a DVD drive, make sure the computer you buy has one.

Screen Size

When you're using a computer, you'll spend a lot of time staring at the screen, so it's a good idea to make sure that you get one that's big enough to read comfortably. Keep in mind, though, that the bigger the screen, the bulkier and less portable the computer will be. Screen sizes are measured diagonally in inches, just like TV screens. Most desktops have screens between 20" and 27". Most laptops are between 11" and 18", while most tablets are between 7" and 13". If you want to take your laptop on frequent trips, a 13" screen is ideal. If you don't mind leaving your computer at home and want to avoid straining your eyes, you should find a 20" to 24" screen very comfortable.

Operating System

An operating system is like a manager in your computer who makes sure different programs are running properly. All computers need operating systems to function. Most new computers, except those sold by Apple, will already have Windows 10 as their operating system, but it's worth checking to make sure. This book assumes that you have a computer with Windows 10 as its operating system.

There are two versions of Windows 10: Home and Professional. The Professional version includes a few additional features for advanced users, which we won't be covering in this book. It is more expensive, so it's better to look for a computer with Windows 10 Home Edition. But don't worry if you have Professional instead—it can do everything that Home can do, and you'll still be able to follow along with the lessons in this book.

Unboxing Your Computer

Once you have your new desktop, laptop, or tablet, the first step is to take it out of the box and get it all plugged in!

MEETING THE PORTS

The first thing you'll probably notice is some sockets on the back or side of your computer. These sockets, called *ports*, are the connection points for various devices. Think of the power cord for a toaster that you plug into an outlet before you can turn it on. In the same way, you might need to plug a few cables into your computer before you can start to use it.

Let's look at the important ports on your computer and then examine how to insert the cables into the appropriate ports to get connected! Every computer is a little different, and the ports are likely to be in different places on each, but you can see two examples of these ports on a typical computer below. You'll see that not all of these ports are on every computer, and your computer may have other ports not mentioned here. Of course, if your computer is already connected, you can skip this section and go to "Your Main Tools" on page 14.

Power   VGA   HDMI   USB Audio

Power

USB

Audio

HDMI

VGA

* **Power port:** The power port provides the power your computer needs to run. This port is also what you use to charge the battery of a laptop or tablet. We'll take a closer look at the power ports on the three types of computers in "Plugging It In" on page 10.

* **USB port:** A USB port allows you to connect a number of different devices to your computer, such as a keyboard, mouse, printer, USB flash drive, and webcam. For more information about connecting and installing USB devices, see "Connecting a Printer, Scanner, Webcam, or Other Device" on page 293.

* **VGA and HDMI ports:** The VGA and HDMI ports connect your computer to a screen or monitor. If you have a laptop, for example, and you want to watch a movie on a bigger screen, you can use the VGA or HDMI port and cable to connect it to a television.

✳ **Audio ports:** Audio ports let you plug speakers, headphones, and microphones into your computer. On many desktops, these are color coded to help you easily spot the different connections: a green port is used for speakers or headphones and a pink port for microphones. On laptops, you'll probably see a small headphones symbol next to the speaker port and a small microphone symbol next to the microphone port.

PLUGGING IT IN

Now that you're familiar with the various ports on your computer, it's time to start plugging things in! In this section, you'll learn how to connect your computer so you can turn it on. We'll go through each type of computer separately, so you can skip to the section for the computer you have.

Plugging In a Laptop or Tablet

On a laptop or tablet, the plug-in process is quite simple!

1 Plug the power cord into the power port on your laptop or tablet. The power cord should have an outlet plug on one end and a plug that fits in the power port on the other end. The power port on a laptop or tablet is usually circular or rectangular.

2 Plug the outlet end of the power cord into a power outlet.

Your laptop or tablet should now start powering up. If your computer was unplugged and you used some of the battery power, or if you're just not using it at the moment, plug it in like this to recharge the battery.

Plugging In a Desktop

To use a desktop computer, you need the computer tower, a monitor, a mouse, and a keyboard. You'll learn how to connect all of these elements in the next section. If you have any trouble, you should also look at the user manual that came with your computer when you purchased it. This guide should include setup steps specific to your computer.

1 Connect your monitor to your computer using a VGA or HDMI cable.

Connect your monitor to a power outlet using the power cable that came with your monitor.

2 Now get your mouse and keyboard, which should each have a USB cable. Plug your keyboard and mouse into any of the USB ports on your desktop.

If your keyboard or mouse is *wireless*, meaning that it does not have a cable connecting it to the computer, it will come with a small transmitter that connects to a USB port. Find the small device with a USB connection and plug it into any USB port on your computer. A wireless keyboard or mouse will also require batteries. The battery compartment is typically located on the bottom of the keyboard or mouse. There should be a small switch on the bottom of the mouse to turn the mouse on. If you have any other USB devices, such as a printer or webcam, you can connect these to any spare USB ports on your computer as well.

3 If your computer comes with separate speakers, you can usually connect them to your computer's audio port. Otherwise, they might plug into a USB port. Just check the connection at the end of the wire.

4 Connect one end of the power cord to the power port on your computer. Connect the other end of the cord to the outlet on your wall.

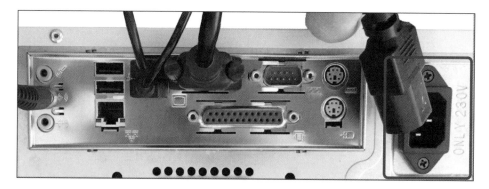

We'll look at turning on the computer shortly, but one thing to know is that if your computer doesn't turn on when you try, it's a good idea to make sure all the plugs are correctly connected. Check that all the plugs are secure in their sockets; some may need to be pushed in fairly hard.

Turning On Your Computer

Your computer will have some sort of power button. The size, shape, and position of power buttons vary between computers, but they will often have a symbol like this: ⏻. If you have trouble finding your power button, you might want to consult the computer's manual or Quick Start Guide.

On a desktop, the power button is usually on the front of the tower. There should also be another power button on the monitor, which needs to be turned on separately. This is usually on the front or side of the monitor screen.

On a laptop, the power button is usually located above the keyboard, as shown next.

On a tablet, the power button is usually on the side or top of the tablet, as shown here.

Power

Your Main Tools

Once your computer is on, you'll need to learn how to give it instructions using the keyboard and mouse.

THE MOUSE

One of your main tools is the *mouse*, shown next. If you have a desktop computer, your mouse will look like the one on the left and should sit next to your computer on the side of your dominant hand. A laptop computer has a *touchpad*, shown on the right, which is a built-in mouse on your keyboard that looks like a pad with two clickable buttons.

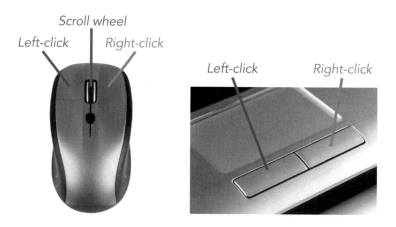

You use the mouse to navigate on the screen. If you watch the screen, you'll notice that as you move your mouse, a small arrow ↖ follows the movements of your hand over the screen. This is called the *pointer*. It lets you select things on your screen to help you control the computer. Depending on the program you're using, that pointer can change to a hand 👆 or a cursor I.

Using the mouse to give commands to your computer is easy!

* **Left-click (usually known as just "click"):** Press once on the left mouse button with your forefinger and immediately release it. This type of click is often used to select something on the screen or to activate a button, as you've already seen.

* **Double-click:** Press on the left button on your mouse twice in quick succession. This type of click is generally used to open an item, such as a program or a folder.

* **Right-click:** Press once on the right button of your mouse and release it. Right-clicking something, or just right-clicking the screen, usually opens a small menu of items. The menu will be different depending on what you right-click.

* **Scroll wheel:** Most mice have a little wheel between the right and left click buttons. Gently rolling the wheel lets you roll up or down the screen so you can see more content.

Tablets come with *touchscreens* that allow you to use your fingers to interact directly with the display without using a device like a mouse. You'll be able to control the pointer by simply touching the screen with your finger! There are four important actions to know:

* **Tap:** A tap involves pressing your finger down once and quickly lifting it. This is the same as a left-click with a mouse. If you're following this book on a touchpad, you can tap whenever you're asked to click.

* **Double-tap:** This involves tapping your finger on a button or region of the screen twice in quick succession. It's equivalent to double-clicking with a mouse.

* **Press and hold:** This involves holding your finger down on a button or region of the screen for a few seconds. This is the same thing as right-clicking with a mouse.

* **Drag:** A drag involves lightly pressing down on the screen with your finger and then moving it to the spot you want while keeping it pressed against the screen. Lift your finger off the screen when you're done moving it to the desired spot. This action is similar to scrolling with a mouse.

You can also use a desktop computer mouse with a laptop, which many people find easier to use than the touchpad, so it's worth trying out both methods. To connect a mouse to your laptop, simply connect the cable attached to the mouse to any spare USB port on your laptop.

THE KEYBOARD

Before you set up your computer, it's worth looking at a few keyboard skills, too. As you'll see in the lessons, pressing a letter or number key on the keyboard places that letter or number on the screen wherever the cursor (I) is located. The following diagram outlines some of the important parts of the keyboard that you'll need to know.

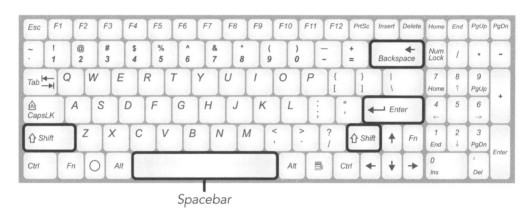

Spacebar

* **Enter key:** Press ENTER to move your cursor down a line or finish inputting information in a text field.

* **Backspace key:** Press BACKSPACE to erase the last letter that you typed. Keeping it held down erases more characters!

* **Shift key:** Hold down SHIFT and press a letter key at the same time to type that letter in uppercase. You can also hold down the SHIFT key and tap a number key at the same time to type the symbol on the number key. For example, holding SHIFT and pressing the number 1 key inserts an exclamation mark!

* **Spacebar:** The spacebar inserts a space. Tap it to make a space between words as you type.

On a tablet, the keyboard appears onscreen when you tap in a box that allows you to type. The onscreen keyboard looks like this:

Numbers key

Shift   Emoticons key   Backspace Enter Shift

Tapping the numbers key changes the onscreen keyboard to display numbers and symbols instead of letters. To change the keyboard back to displaying letters, press the numbers key again. You can also use the emoticons key to insert fun pictures.

Setting Up Your Computer

Now that your computer is on and you know a bit about how to use the main tools to navigate it, it's time to get familiar with Windows 10!

Whether you purchased a new computer or upgraded a computer to use Windows 10 from an older version such as Windows 7 or Windows 8, you'll need to set up your computer. This includes connecting your computer to the internet and setting up a Microsoft account, which you'll use throughout this book. If you don't feel completely confident doing this alone, you can often ask the store where you purchased your computer to set it up for you.

SETTING UP AN INTERNET CONNECTION

It's good to first make sure your computer is connected to the internet because you'll need it for setting up your Microsoft account. The *internet* is a vast community of computers that can communicate with each other.

By connecting to the internet, your computer can talk to other computers and access information added by other users. The internet lets you send messages to friends and family, look up information, read the news, watch videos, get directions, shop and bank online, and much, much more!

Before you can join the internet, you need to sign up with an *internet service provider (ISP)*, which will be the company connecting you to the internet in the same way your phone company connects you to other phones. Here are some common ISPs in the US:

* Comcast

* AT&T

* Spectrum

* CenturyLink

* Verizon

There are two main types of internet connection. *Fixed* internet connections let you use the internet at home and usually allow unlimited use for a set monthly fee. *Mobile* internet connections let you use the internet when you're out and about but only provide you with a limited amount of usage each month, so you won't be able to view as many pages, emails, and videos. You should discuss your needs with an ISP, and be prepared to shop around for a good price.

If you're not ready to take the leap just yet, you can always visit a friend or relative who has an internet connection, or visit your local library and connect to the internet there.

CONNECTING TO THE INTERNET

When you first turn on your computer, you should see a setup screen. Some computer manufacturers add their own steps and screens as well, so the choices you see on your computer might not exactly match the ones pictured but should be similar. If your computer has already been set up, you can skip ahead to Lesson 1.

If you're not already connected to the internet when you start the setup process, you'll be asked to connect first before anything else. You should see a list of available nearby internet connections. To connect to the internet, follow these steps:

1 Click the internet connection you want to use. If you've signed up for internet, your ISP will have provided you with the network name you should connect to.

2 Enter the password to the connection, if you're asked for one. This should also have been provided by your ISP. It's usually also printed on the underside of your modem router so you can find it easily.

3 Click **Connect**.

CHOOSING YOUR KEYBOARD SETTINGS

Your next step is to choose your region and keyboard settings.

1 Windows will select the region it thinks you're in. If the selected region is correct, simply click **Yes**. Otherwise, click the region you're in, such as United States, before clicking Yes.

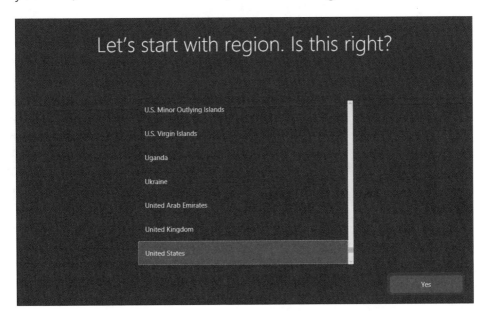

2 Windows will ask which keyboard layout you're using, because different countries often have different types of keyboards. Click the region in which you bought your keyboard and then click **Yes**. If you're not sure, just click Yes without choosing a different layout.

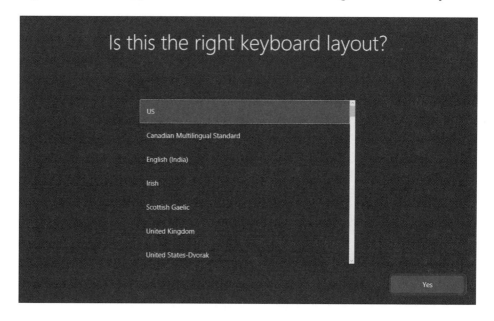

3 You'll then be asked if you want to add a second keyboard layout. Most people don't need this, so click **Skip**.

CREATING A MICROSOFT ACCOUNT

The next step is to create a Microsoft account, which will provide you with an email address and let you install apps on your computer. We'll make use of these features throughout this book, so it is important to set up a Microsoft account now.

If you have an email address that ends in *@outlook.com* or *@hotmail.com*, you already have a Microsoft account. In this case, you can simply enter your email address and the password for that email account in the boxes shown and then click **Sign in**. If you have a Microsoft account but have forgotten your password, click the **Forgotten your password?** button and then follow the instructions on the screen to reset it. Next, skip ahead to "Managing Your Advertising Options" on page 24.

If you don't have a Microsoft account, click **Create account** and then follow the directions provided in the next sections.

Creating an Email Address

The first thing your new Microsoft account must have is an email address. If you already have a non-Microsoft email address, such as a Gmail or Yahoo address, you can enter it here, click **Next**, and then skip ahead to "Creating a Password" on page 22. If you don't have an email address, you need to create one. Continue with these steps to do so:

1. Click **Get a new email address** to create a new address.

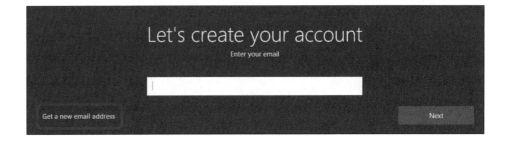

2 Now you need to create a unique name for your new email address! No one else in the world can use the same email address; if they could, emails sent to that address would go to both of you. You might need to be creative to find one that hasn't been used before. You can use any combination of letters and numbers, but your new address has to end in *@outlook.com*. Be sure to write down your new email address because you'll need it later. Once you've typed in your new email address, click the **Next** button.

Creating a Password

Whether you used an existing email address or just created a new one, you'll also need to choose a password.

> ✱ **NOTE:** *Make sure you choose a password you can remember—you'll need to type it in every time you use your computer. It's probably a good idea to write it down somewhere safe as well.*

To keep your Microsoft account safe, use a unique password that you don't use for anything else. Your password must be at least eight characters long and should include numbers and letters, to make it harder to guess. Good passwords do not include factual information that others know about you (such as your name or birthday) or personal details that others will easily guess (such as your pet or best friend's name). You should also avoid well-known phrases or letters such as "abc123" and "good morning."

1 Click in the **Password** box and enter a new password.

2 Click **Next**.

Entering Personal Information

You'll need to enter a few more personal details to continue. This is required for Microsoft to comply with child privacy legislation and is perfectly safe to provide. Note that if you're located outside of the United States, you won't be asked for your date of birth.

1 Click in the **Location** box and choose your country from the drop-down list.

2 Click in the **Birthdate** box and choose the date you were born in the format requested: usually month, then day, then year.

3 Click **Next**.

Providing a Phone Number for Security Information

If you ever forget your password and need to reset it, Microsoft can call you or send you a text message to make sure it's really you and not a hacker trying to get into your account!

1 Select your country from the drop-down box.

2 Enter your phone number (with the area code) in the field to the right of the drop-down box.

3 Click **Next**.

MANAGING YOUR ADVERTISING OPTIONS

Microsoft should now ask your permission to use your information when deciding what type of advertising to show you. This is quite safe, but if you don't want Microsoft to do this, uncheck the **Enhance my online experiences...** box. If you don't want any special offers to be emailed to you by Microsoft, you can also uncheck the **Send me promotional offers from Microsoft** box. Click **Next** to move on.

SKIPPING PIN SETUP

Microsoft also encourages you to set a personal identification number (PIN), as well as a password, that you can use to sign in to your computer. This can make it a bit faster to log in to your computer, but it's also one more number to memorize. Rather than adding yet another password to your list, click **Do this later**.

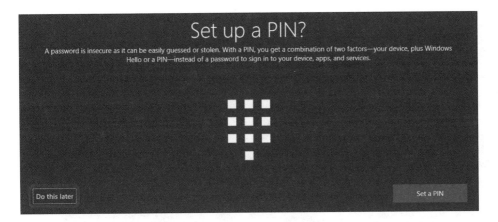

SKIPPING ONEDRIVE SETUP

Microsoft encourages you to save all your documents and pictures to OneDrive, which is a storage area online. This can be handy, as you'll see when we look at setting up OneDrive in Lesson 13, but for now, click **No**.

YOUR OWN DIGITAL ASSISTANT: CORTANA!

Microsoft wants to introduce you to its digital assistant, Cortana. Cortana lets you give verbal directions to your computer, like "Open the News app" or "Search for pictures of cats." We won't cover these verbal directions in this book, but there's no harm in having Cortana available, so click **Yes**.

PRIVACY SETTINGS

Finally, you'll be asked to choose some privacy settings that control the type of information you share with Microsoft. The default settings are quite safe, and they allow you to make full use of the new Windows 10 features, but if you aren't comfortable sharing any of this information with Microsoft, you can click any of the sliders to change the setting from On to Off (in the case of diagnostics, from Full to Basic). When you're satisfied with the privacy settings, click **Accept**.

Your computer might take a few minutes to finish processing your settings, but this concludes the setup process.

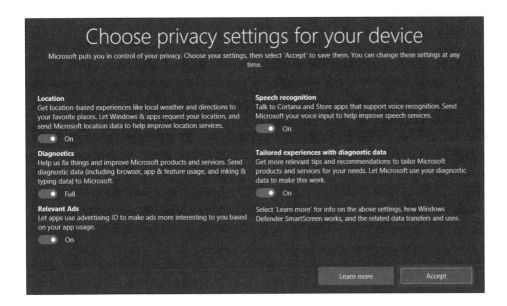

Phew, We Did It!

We've looked at buying and setting up a computer and examined the different types of computers and their most important specifications. We also looked at the different types of internet connections and how to connect to the internet. You learned how to do the following:

* Choose which computer type is best for you

* Unbox and plug in your new computer

* Decide what type of internet connection is right for you

* Turn on your computer

* Use the keyboard and mouse

* Set up Windows 10 on your new computer

* Connect to the internet

Great work! Now that your computer is set up, move on to Lesson 1 to start using it.

LESSON 1
GETTING STARTED

Welcome to your computer!

In this lesson, you'll start using your computer and get familiar with its home screen so you can start using it with confidence. You'll learn how to turn your computer on and log in. You'll also practice using your mouse to navigate around and open and close an app. Finally, you'll see how to turn your computer off.

> ✱ **NOTE:** *This lesson assumes you've already set up your computer. If you haven't done so, flip back to "Setting Up Your Computer" on page 17 and follow the instructions there.*

Starting Your Computer

To start using your computer, turn it on by pressing the power button. Once your computer has loaded, the first thing you should see is the *lock screen*, like the one shown here.

3:05
Thursday, June 1

This is a safety screen intended to stop anyone from accessing your computer until they've typed in the correct password. Because the lock screen doesn't show any personal information, strangers won't be able to see anything personal about you if they happen to sit down at your computer.

LOGGING IN

You should already have created a Microsoft account in "Setting Up Your Computer" on page 17, and you can use it now to log in to your computer.

1 From the lock screen, click the left mouse button (referred to from here on out as a *click*) or press any key on the keyboard.

2 This brings up the name you used to create your account and an empty box underneath. This is where you'll enter your password. Move your mouse over this empty password box and click it once.

3 Type the password you created when you first installed Windows. You should type this in carefully because you won't be able to move past the lock screen until you've entered the correct password. As you type, the characters will appear as dots, but don't worry: this is just to stop anyone nearby from seeing what your password is while you type it.

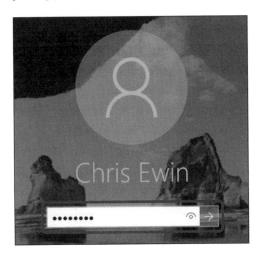

4   If you do want to see what you've entered to make sure you've typed in your password correctly, click the ☞ symbol to reveal the letters.

5   Once you've typed in your password, press ENTER on your keyboard or click the arrow button to the right of the password box.

6   The computer will then load for a few more moments. If you entered your password incorrectly, you will have the chance to type it in again.

Once you've successfully logged in, you'll be taken to your *desktop*; this is your "mission control." The desktop is the main screen you'll use to navigate to other areas of your computer.

> **✳ NOTE:** *The word* desktop *has been used to mean two different things so far. A desktop computer, like the one we talked about in "What Kind of Computer Do I Need?" on page 2, is a computer that sits on your desk. Your desktop screen, shown on the next page, is the main starting screen. You'll get the hang of the difference very quickly!*

NAVIGATING THE DESKTOP

Your computer is now fired up, and you should be at the desktop screen. This is where you can find and open useful apps that will help you do things such as send emails, play games, view photos, use the internet, make video calls, and much, much more. This is also where you can find important tools you'll use all the time.

Let's take a closer look at the desktop screen and some of its most useful components. (If you're using a Windows tablet and your screen doesn't look like this, see "Navigating a Windows Tablet" on page 36.)

Desktop background

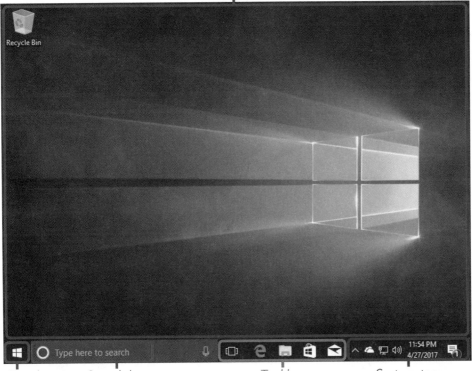

Start button Search box   Taskbar   System tray

The Desktop Background

The striking image you see on the desktop is a backdrop for your main screen, so whenever you have nothing else open on your computer, this is what you'll see.

The desktop is a handy place to quickly access apps, games, and documents that you use often. You can access these things by using the small pictures, known as *icons*, on the desktop. You'll notice in the figure above that an icon for the Recycle Bin has been included on Windows 10. The Recycle Bin holds any documents that you delete from your computer (hence it looks like a bin!). Because you might use this frequently, the icon for the Recycle Bin is on your desktop for quick and easy access. You'll learn more about the Recycle Bin in Lesson 13.

The Start Button

Clicking the start button brings up the Start menu, which is a list of all the apps stored on your computer. The Start menu will probably be your main method of finding and opening programs, apps, documents, and so on, so you'll use it a lot throughout this book.

The Search Box

The search box helps you search for things on your computer or on the internet. You type in a word or phrase connected with what you want to find, and Windows will try to find matches. We'll explore how to use the search box in just a moment, but don't be concerned if you don't see the search box on your screen.

The Taskbar

The taskbar is the dark bar that runs along the bottom of your screen, and it should be visible even when you open other apps and documents. You can save shortcuts to a few of your favorite or most frequently used apps here, and they will appear as icons. Just like desktop icons, the aim of the icons on the taskbar is to give you quick access to your favorite apps. To open programs using the taskbar, simply click the icon.

The System Tray

The system tray gives you information about the status of your computer, such as whether you are connected to the internet. You don't need to worry about the system tray too much, but there are a few useful items you might want to know about.

The system tray is home to the volume control . This lets you adjust the volume of your computer. The number of "waves" next to the icon gives you an idea of how loud the volume is set. One wave indicates the volume is set quite low, whereas three waves indicate that the volume is quite high, like in the image above. An X next to the icon lets you know that the volume has been muted. To adjust the volume, move your mouse over the volume control icon and click it just once. A slider will pop up. You can click the slider and, while holding the left mouse button down, drag the slider up or down to raise or lower the volume.

The system tray also has a clock, which displays the time and date. Clicking the clock once will display a mini calendar, like the one shown here. You can go forward or backward in time by clicking the small arrow pointing up or down, respectively.

On the far right side of the system tray is a *notifications* icon . This shows you any recent messages that Windows thinks are important, such as new emails you've received (see Lesson 4). In this image, the small number 1 next to the notifications icon lets us know that we have one new Windows message, and if we click the icon, we'll be able to see what that message is.

Many of the icons in the system tray are hidden from view. This is because most of the icons that live in the system tray are programs that work behind the scenes, and you won't need to think about them much. If you want to explore these hidden icons, you can click the small up arrow on the left of the system tray .

To find out the name of one of these programs, you can hover over the icon with your mouse, without clicking, and a small box will pop up with the name of the program.

NAVIGATING A WINDOWS TABLET

A Windows tablet works in a very similar way to a Windows computer, with a few differences. Depending on the manufacturer, your tablet might be set to *tablet mode*, which changes the size and position of some buttons to make them easier for you to tap with a finger. We'll show you how to turn tablet mode on and off at the end of this section.

The Start Screen

The Start screen is the first screen you'll see after you turn on your tablet. It is a launching pad to help you do everything else on your tablet. Just like the Start menu on a desktop or laptop computer, the Start screen offers you a list of all the apps and helps you search for particular apps.

Popular apps button
Full apps list button
Popular apps tiles

Start button, Back button, Search button, Task view button

System tray

Let's explore the Start screen in more detail.

- ✳ **Popular apps tiles:** These apps come on all Windows 10 tablets and appear as small tiles in the middle of the Start screen. Learn more in "The Popular Apps Tiles" on page 40.

- ✳ **Full apps list button:** Tapping this button will open a list of all the apps on your tablet. This list is the same as the full apps list on the Start menu of a desktop or laptop computer. Flip to "The Full Apps List" on page 39 to learn more.

- ✳ **Start button:** Tapping this button will take you straight to the Start screen, regardless of what you were doing a moment ago. If you tap the start button from the Start screen, then the Start screen will disappear and return you to the app you were using before.

- ✳ **Back button:** This button will take you back to the screen you were looking at one tap ago. So if you've opened a web page, an app, or a document, this button will take you back to the page you were looking at before. You can keep tapping this button to go back until you reach the Start screen.

- ✳ **Search button:** This button will help you find apps or files on your tablet. See "Using the Search Box" on page 41 for more information on how to search for an app.

- ✳ **Task view button:** This button will show you all the apps, web pages, and documents currently open on your tablet. Tap this button to see small images of everything currently open and tap the image to open that particular app, web page, or document.

- ✳ **System tray:** The bottom-right corner of the screen shows you information about important settings on your tablet (like your internet connection). Learn more about the system tray in "The System Tray" on page 34.

Turning Tablet Mode On and Off

The screenshots and steps in this book focus on computers rather than tablets. Have no fear! You'll easily be able to follow along in tablet mode by staying aware of the few differences mentioned above. Fortunately, you can also go one step further and set your tablet to look exactly like a computer by following the steps below. Many manufacturers sell their tablets set up like computers, so you might find your tablet is already set up this way!

1 Tap the **notification center** icon from the system tray.

2 You should see the "Tablet mode" button on the left. If it's blue, like the one highlighted below, your device is set to display as a tablet.

3 If you tap the **Tablet mode** button, it will change to gray and your tablet will display like a desktop or laptop computer.

4 Tap the icon a second time to turn tablet mode back on.

If you decide to use your tablet with tablet mode turned off, your screen will look like the one shown on page 33 and you'll open and search for apps using the Start menu, described next.

Finding Apps from the Start Menu

Now that you're familiar with the desktop, you'll learn how to open an app! *App* is a broad term that refers to a tool for doing something specific on your computer. For example, the Microsoft Solitaire Collection app lets you play a card game, and the WordPad app lets you write a letter. Note that in older versions of Windows, you may have heard these referred to as *programs*.

To open an app, follow these steps:

1 Click the **start button** in the bottom-left corner of the screen.

2 This brings up the Start menu. Apps are shown in two ways: as a list on the left and as an array of picture tiles on the right.

Full apps list   *Popular apps tiles*

✱ *NOTE: You can click anywhere outside of the Start menu to close it.*

Let's look at these two app views in more detail next.

THE FULL APPS LIST

The apps list on the left side of the Start menu is a collection of icons for all of the apps on your computer, listed alphabetically. If you move your mouse pointer into the list of apps, a gray bar will appear, as highlighted next.

This bar (known as a *scroll bar*) lets you move up and down through the list to see more apps. Click the down arrow at the bottom of the scroll bar and hold down the mouse button to move down the list of apps. If your mouse has a scroll wheel, you can move your cursor over the list and, without clicking, roll the scroll wheel up or down to move through the list. You can open any of these apps simply by clicking it once.

Scroll bar

Folders

Some apps in the list are grouped into *folders*, indicated with a folder icon. For example, if you scroll down the list of apps to *W*, you should see a folder named *Windows Accessories*. The WordPad app, a handy program for writing letters, is stored inside this *Windows Accessories* folder. To find WordPad, click the **Windows Accessories** folder to open it and then you should see a list of apps that includes the WordPad icon. Don't click it yet; we'll look at using it in Lesson 12.

THE POPULAR APPS TILES

On the right side of the Start menu, you can see a number of larger tiles for the more popular apps, such as Calendar, Mail, Weather, and Photos. You can open any of these apps by clicking the tile once.

Some apps show current information in real time, so they will look slightly different each time you open the Start menu. For example, the icon for the Weather app might show you the current temperature in your location, whereas the icon for the Photos app might show you a recent photo you've put on your computer. But don't worry—you'll still be able to recognize an app by its name and the nature of the image shown!

ACTIVITY #1

In this activity, you'll practice finding an app using the Start menu.

1. Open the Start menu.

2. Find the Weather app in the popular apps tiles. But don't click it yet! We'll look at opening and using this app in Lesson 2.

3. Find the Weather app in the full apps list.

4. Close the Start menu.

USING THE SEARCH BOX

Finding apps by scrolling through the entire menu can take a long time, and if the app you're looking for is stored in a folder, then it may be tricky to find! Fortunately, there is a quicker way to find apps. If you know the name of the app you want, then you can enter the name into the search box at the bottom of the screen, shown here. Depending on your settings, this button might appear as a circle without any words.

Your computer will then search for the app for you! The description in the search box may change depending on your settings. For example, your search box might read "Ask my anything" or "Search the web and Windows," but it won't make any difference to your search. If you don't see the search box, don't panic! Your search box may have been hidden, and it will appear when you begin your search.

Whether you see the box or not, follow these steps to search for an app:

1   Click inside the search box. This brings up a larger search box where you type in the name of the app you want to open. If you don't see the search box, click the start button. This won't bring up the search box straight away, but you'll see it as soon as you type a letter.

2   Type in the word **calculator**. As you type, Windows immediately begins giving you suggestions by trying to complete the word.

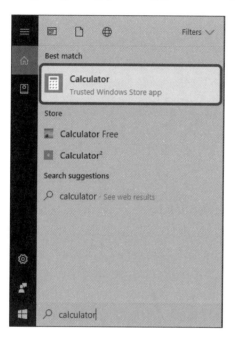

3   Once you see the name of your app in the suggestions, you can stop typing. You should see the Calculator app appear at the top under "Best match."

Using Your First App

Now let's open the Calculator app we just searched for. The Calculator app lets you add, subtract, and perform other calculations easily.

OPENING THE APP

Follow these steps to open the Calculator app:

1 Click the **Calculator app icon** from the list of search results. You can also find the Calculator app from the full apps list.

2 The Calculator app should appear on your screen.

3 Click the calculator buttons to begin a calculation. For example, you can enter the number 10 by clicking the **1** button followed by the **0** button. Then click the multiplication sign and enter another number for the calculation. When you've finished entering the calculation, click **=** to see the result displayed at the top of the calculator screen.

* TIP: *You can also enter numbers into the Calculator app using the keyboard rather than clicking the onscreen buttons. Give it a go!*

MAXIMIZING AN APP

You might find that an app is too small to see properly, in which case you can *maximize* it. Maximizing an app allows it to take up the full screen. To do so, simply click the **maximize button** in the top-right corner of your app, as shown here.

Your app will now take up the whole screen. Note that the maximize button now looks like this: ⬚. Click this button again to return the app to its previous size.

CLOSING AN APP

Closing an app will exit the app and take you back to the desktop. You should always close apps when you have finished using them, because having too many apps open at the same time can slow your computer down. Most apps will have a small button in the top-right corner with an X on it. Click this **close button** to make the app disappear from your screen!

On a tablet, you can close an app by dragging your finger from the top of the screen to the bottom. You can also move your finger to the top right of the screen and the close button will appear.

ACTIVITY #2

In this activity, you'll practice opening and closing the News app.

1. Open the News app.

2. Choose your country to load news relevant to you, and click an article to read it.

3. Maximize the News app window.

4. When you have finished reading the article, close the News app.

RESTORING DISAPPEARING APPS

If you clicked somewhere outside your app and your app disappeared, don't worry! You probably didn't close the app, but just *minimized* it. Minimizing hides the app from main view to prevent cluttering your screen, but you can bring it back easily! You can minimize an app yourself by clicking the minimize button, highlighted here.

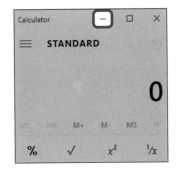

Follow these steps to open your app again:

1   Find your taskbar running along the bottom of your screen.

2   In the taskbar, look for the icon of the app you want to bring back. For example, the Calculator app icon will look like a calculator. You should see a small blue line underneath the app icon, which tells you that it is currently open. If the line isn't there, it means the app has been closed, and you can open it again through the Start menu, as you did earlier in this lesson.

3   Click the icon.

4   The Calculator app should now be visible!

If you can't find the Calculator app icon in the taskbar, it's likely that the app has been closed. To reopen the app, you will need to find it again from the Start menu. You can also display a list of your currently open apps by clicking the Task View button. Find the app you want to restore and click it.

> *** NOTE:** *If you click the taskbar icon of an app that's currently visible on the screen, it will also minimize it! Click the icon a second time to bring the app back up on the screen.*

Shutting Down Your Computer

Shutting down your computer turns it off. It is a good idea to shut down your computer once you've finished using it, as it saves power. Before you shut down your computer, though, it's important to close any apps that are currently open. If you shut down the computer without closing the apps, you could lose the information or in-progress work in your open apps. To shut down your computer properly, follow these steps:

1   Using the close button, close any apps that are open.

2   Click the **start button** in the bottom-left corner.

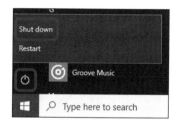

3   From the left side of the Start menu, click the **power button** and then click **Shut down**, as shown here.

Your computer will now shut down. Be aware that this might take a moment.

Phew, We Did It!

In this lesson, we looked at getting started with your computer. You practiced using a mouse to navigate various components of your desktop. We looked at different ways to open and close apps, using the Calculator app as an example. In this lesson, you learned how to do the following:

* Log in to your computer

* Explore the desktop

* Open apps using the Start menu (or Start screen) and using the search box

* Use the Calculator app

* Maximize apps

* Close apps

* Minimize and restore apps

* Shut down your computer

In the next lesson, you'll learn more about some popular apps: Solitaire, Weather, and Calendar.

LESSON REVIEW

Congratulations! You've completed Lesson 1. Take this opportunity to review what you've learned by completing the following tasks. If you can complete all these tasks with confidence, then you are ready for Lesson 2. If not, don't lose heart—just keep practicing!

1. Turn on your computer.

2. Log in using your password.

3. Find the Calculator app.

4. Open the Calculator app.

5. Use the Calculator app to find out the answer to 10 + 12.

6. Close the Calculator app.

LESSON 2

INTRODUCING APPS

In this lesson, you'll unlock the true power of your computer by learning to use apps!

What Is an App?

An *app* (short for *application*) is a tool on your computer that helps you do a specific job, like play a game or check the weather. You might also have heard it referred to as a *program*. Apps make it easier and faster to do the things you want to do on your computer. Your computer already has a lot of great apps on it that you can use to do the following:

* Play music

* Play movies

* Manage your photos

* Chat with friends and family

* Keep track of your appointments

* Play games

* Read the latest news

* And much, much more

You already met the Calculator app in Lesson 1. Now we'll explore some other popular and useful apps on your computer. First, you'll use the Microsoft Solitaire Collection app to play different types of solitaire games. Then you'll use the Weather app to check the weather forecast and the Calendar app to help you track appointments and events. By the end of this lesson, you should feel confident to explore the other apps on your computer at your leisure.

> *** NOTE:** *Some of the apps we'll be exploring, such as the Weather app, require you to be connected to the internet. If you're not yet online, flip back to "Setting Up an Internet Connection" on page 17 to see more about getting connected.*

DID SOMEONE SAY FREE?

All the apps already on your computer are free to use and enjoy! However, a few of them may offer you the opportunity to buy items; for example, the Movies and TV app will let you play your own videos for free but will offer you the opportunity to buy television shows and movies. Don't be concerned, though: you can't accidentally buy something in an app! If something has to be paid for, you'll be given plenty of warning, and you would need to enter your credit card details to make a payment. In this lesson, we're going to focus on learning about the completely free apps, starting with Solitaire.

The Microsoft Solitaire Collection App

Solitaire is one of the most popular free game apps and can provide hours of fun. Your Windows 10 computer comes with a range of solitaire games in the Microsoft Solitaire Collection app. If you're not a solitaire fan, don't worry: we'll explore how to add more games in Lesson 8. But first, to get you used to using apps, let's explore the Solitaire Collection.

1   Click the **start button** in the bottom-left corner of the screen, highlighted here.

2   The Start menu will appear. Click the tile that says **Microsoft Solitaire Collection**, highlighted next.

3 If you don't see this tile in the Start menu, use the search feature to find it. Click in the search box next to the start button and then type **solitaire**. Click **Microsoft Solitaire Collection** from the list that appears.

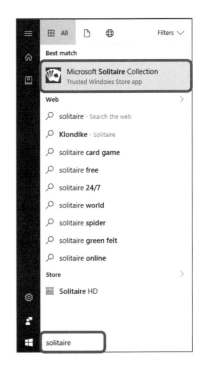

4 The app will then open on your screen! It should look something like this:

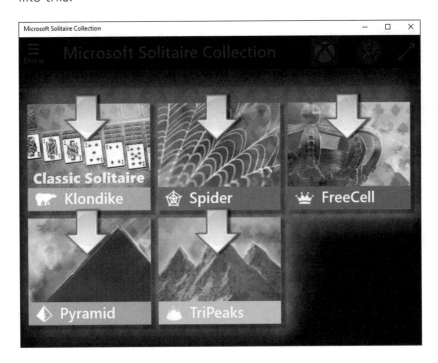

Now, let's play the game!

PLAYING A GAME

The Microsoft Solitaire Collection includes five different versions of solitaire to choose from:

* Klondike (also known as Classic Solitaire)

* Spider

* FreeCell

* Pyramid

* TriPeaks

Let's start by playing everybody's favorite . . . Klondike!

1 Click the **Klondike** button.

2 A small help screen will appear, offering to tell you how to play.

3 If you're not familiar with Klondike, you can read the "How to play"
guide by clicking the **Next** button. Once you've finished reading
this guide, click **Play the game** to jump in! If you know the game
well, check the **Do not show again** box and then click **Close**, and
you'll be taken straight to the game.

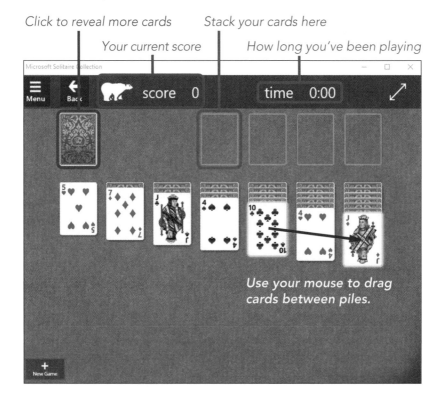

Click to reveal more cards *Stack your cards here*

Your current score *How long you've been playing*

Use your mouse to drag
cards between piles.

The aim of Klondike is to stack all the cards in their individual suits, from ace to king, in the empty slots at the top right. To move a card to a stack, move your mouse cursor over a card, click and hold down your left mouse button, move your mouse over the appropriate pile, and then release the mouse button. You start a stack by moving an ace to any of the empty slots.

You can also move cards between the columns at the bottom to reveal new cards. You do this in the same way, by holding down your left mouse button on a card and dragging it to a new pile. In the lower columns, cards must be placed in descending order, alternating red and black cards. For example, in the image above, the black 10 can be moved onto the red jack, but cannot be placed on top of the black jack.

Click once on the deck in the top-left corner to reveal three fresh cards from the deck. You can move only the top card of these three, by clicking the card and dragging it to a column or stack.

Click the double-headed arrow in the top-right corner to make the game take up the entire screen. When the game takes up the entire screen, you can click the button again to make it smaller.

If you get stuck and want to start a new game, click the **New Game** button in the bottom-left corner to start again with a fresh deck of cards.

CLOSING A GAME

You can close Microsoft Solitaire Collection in the same way you closed the Calculator app in Lesson 1. Click the **close button** in the top-right corner, as shown here. This will take you back to the Desktop.

If you close this app after starting but not completing a game, your session will be automatically saved. That way, when you open the app again, the game will pick up at the same place as your last session. This allows you to finish the game the next time you open the app!

If you'd like to try a different version of solitaire, simply click the **Back** button in the top-left corner of the screen and choose a different game.

OPENING SOLITAIRE AGAIN

The first time you open Microsoft Solitaire Collection, you'll be able to play the game right away. When you open the app for a second time, however, you might be asked to create an Xbox profile, as shown next. This lets you track your scores and share your progress with friends online.

If this appeals to you, click **Next** and follow the prompts. However, if you just want to play the game, click **Not now**. The Microsoft Solitaire Collection app will ask you if you're really sure about this, so check the box that says **Don't show this again** and click **Play as a Guest**.

No Microsoft Account

By signing in with a Microsoft Account, you will have access to Xbox Live Achievements, Leaderboards, and your game data will be saved in the cloud. Are you sure?

Don't show this again   **Sign in**   **Play as a Guest**

Now you can choose your favorite type of solitaire just as before and begin playing.

ACTIVITY #3

In this activity, you'll try another game in the Microsoft Solitaire Collection!

1. Open **Microsoft Solitaire Collection** using the Start menu.

2. Open the **Spider** game.

3. Play through a complete game of Spider solitaire.

4. Close the Microsoft Solitaire Collection app.

The Weather App

Now let's have a look at the Weather app. The Weather app tells you the current weather for any location you choose. It also shows you a forecast for the next few days so that you can plan accordingly. Remember that you need to be connected to the internet to use the Weather app. Let's start by opening the Weather app:

1. Click the **start button** in the bottom-left corner of the screen.

2 The Start menu will open, and you should see a tile with a white sun that's labeled **Weather**, as shown next. (Your Weather tile might show the current temperature instead of a white sun.) Click this tile to open the Weather app.

3 If you don't see the Weather app in the Start menu, use the search feature. Click in the search box next to the start button and type **weather**. Click **Weather** from the list that appears.

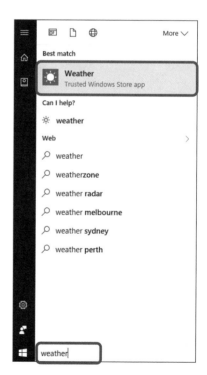

4 If this is the first time you've opened the Weather app, you'll see a screen like the one shown here.

5 Click either Fahrenheit or Celsius, whichever is your preference.

6 The Weather app will also ask you to set your default city. When you open the Weather app in the future, it will automatically give you the weather for your default city, so it's often best to use your own location for this. You can do this by either letting Windows detect your location or selecting a location yourself.

7 To let Windows detect your location, click **Detect my location**. You'll then be asked to give the Weather app permission to access your location. Click **Yes**.

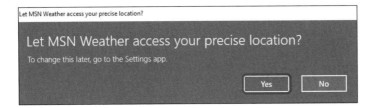

8 If you prefer not to let the app access your location information, you can instead click in the Search box below the "Detect my location" button and type the name of your city.

9 Click **Start** to save this information.

The Weather app should now open, showing you the weather forecast for your current city, set out like the following figure.

Current weather in your default city

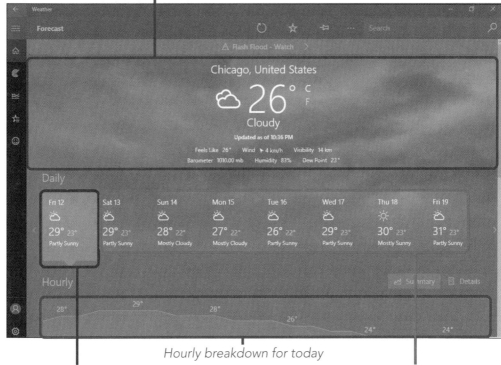

Today's weather with highs and lows

Hourly breakdown for today

Forecast for the next seven days

The Weather app will tell you the current temperature along with some key facts, such as the wind speed and humidity. This information is shown above the forecast for the next few days. Below the daily forecasts, you'll see a breakdown of the hourly temperature for the rest of the day, with a line showing how the temperature will change. You can even scroll down further to see more details, such as when the sun will rise and set!

The Calendar App

Another handy app on your computer is the Calendar app. The Calendar app helps you keep track of appointments, birthdays, vacations, and other important events. It's like having a daily planner on your computer. Better still, the Calendar app can display a small notification to remind you that your event or appointment is about to start. Now that's an assistant worth having!

SETTING UP THE CALENDAR APP

To open the Calendar app, follow these steps:

1 Click the **start button** in the bottom-left corner of the screen.

2 The Start menu will open, and you should see the Calendar app tile. It might show the word "Calendar" or the current date. Click the **Calendar** tile.

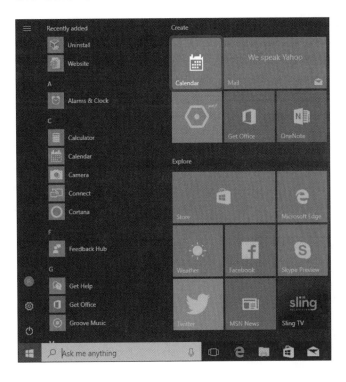

3 If you don't see the Calendar app in the Start menu, use the search feature. Click in the search box next to the start button and type **calendar**. Click **Calendar** from the list that appears.

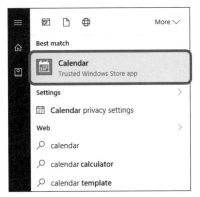

4   Click **Get started**.

5   If this is the first time you've used the Calendar app, you'll be prompted to add an account or use your existing account. The Calendar app uses your account to attribute appointments and events to you. You'll use the same Microsoft account you set up in "Creating a Microsoft Account" on page 20. This account should appear at the top of the Accounts list, so just click **Ready to go**.

If you don't see your account here, you are probably using a local account instead of a Microsoft account. Consult "Switching to a Microsoft Account" on page 297 to learn how to create a Microsoft account.

This will open your personal calendar!

MEETING THE CALENDAR APP

Now that the Calendar app is set up, it's time to start organizing your days. Let's take a look at the main Calendar screen.

Today's date will be shaded in blue. On the left side you'll see a mini calendar that gives you a bird's-eye view of the month. You can use this to peek at future or past months while still keeping your main calendar on today.

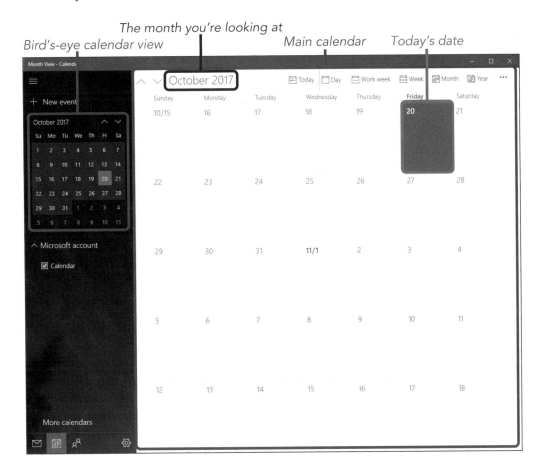

Your calendar isn't restricted to the current month; you can move back and forth through the months to see future and past appointments and events.

To move through the calendar, use these buttons:

Bird's-eye calendar view arrows

Monthly view arrows

Today

* **Monthly view arrows:** Click the up arrow to go back a month and the down arrow to go forward a month.

* **Today:** Click this button to quickly get back to the current date.

* **Bird's-eye calendar view arrows:** Click these arrows to scroll through the bird's-eye calendar view by using the arrows highlighted in the following figure.

Once you're comfortable moving through the calendar to different dates, it's time to move on to adding events.

ADDING AN EVENT

The Calendar app is an excellent place to store information about important events and appointments you want to keep track of. You'll be able to easily view all of your upcoming events, add new events, and even receive reminders before an event starts. That beats a wall calendar! Here's how to add an event:

1 Click the **New event** button, highlighted here.

2 The Calendar app will open a form that asks for some information about the event, with boxes for the event name, location, start and end times, and any extra details. You don't have to fill out all this information, but it is a good idea to have at least an event name and a start date and time.

Event name

Location

Start date and time

End date and time

Event description

✱ **Event name:** Click in the box that contains the words "Event name" (these words will disappear once you begin to type). Type a name for the event (for example, "Doctor's Appointment"). Make it something short but recognizable, because this will appear in the little box for the appropriate day in your main calendar!

✱ **Location:** You can store the location of the event so it can remind you where you need to be. Click in the **Location** box and type the event's location. This could be a full address or simply a helpful reminder, such as "Mary's House."

* **Start date and time:** Select the date of the event or, if your event is longer than one day, the date the event starts. You can type in the date or click the small calendar symbol next to the date (highlighted next) to choose from a list. Remember to click the up or down arrow to cycle through the months if necessary.

Select a start time for the event by clicking the down arrow next to the time and choosing from the list of times. You might need to scroll down a little to find the appropriate time. If your event starts at a specific time that isn't shown, you can type it in, but make sure to type in whether it's AM or PM. Otherwise, it might appear at the wrong time! You can also check the **All day** box if the event will take up the entire day or if you would prefer not to specify an exact time.

* **End date and time:** Choose the date and time your event finishes. If you don't choose an end date or time, the calendar will automatically make the event half an hour long from the start date and time.

* **Event description:** If there are any more details you want to add, you can type them in this field.

Adding a Reminder

The Calendar app can remind you of an event with a small box that pops up in the corner of your computer screen just before your event begins and gives you a summary of the event details. This box will appear regardless of whether you have the Calendar app open at that particular time. This way, you won't forget appointments during your busy day.

Here's how to add a reminder:

1 Click in the **Reminder** box, as shown here.

2 Choose when you want to be reminded about the event. For example, a 30-minute reminder will let you know 30 minutes in advance of the start time of the event.

✱ **NOTE:** *When the reminder box pops up, you can close it by clicking the **Dismiss** button. Alternatively, you can click the **Snooze** button to be reminded about the event again in a few minutes' time.*

Saving Your Event

After you've set your event details, it's time to save the event. Simply click the **Save and close** button to save your details and your reminder.

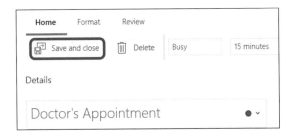

You'll now be returned to the main calendar screen. Your event should appear in a shaded blue strip on the appropriate date, like in the following figure. This shaded strip will show only a snippet of the information. To see the full details of any event, just click it once with your mouse.

> ✱ *TIP: You can also create an event by clicking the appropriate box for the date of your event; this will bring up a mini version of the "New event" form, like in the figure shown next. Either add a few details here or click **More details** to bring up the full form.*

DELETING AN EVENT

If an event has been canceled or if you no longer need it on your calendar, you can remove it. Here's how to delete an event:

1   Find the event in your calendar and right-click the shaded blue strip.

2   Click the **Delete** button, shown next.

The event will now disappear from your calendar.

ACTIVITY #4

Let's practice adding events to your calendar:

1. Add the birthdays of your closest friends and family members to the calendar.

2. Add any important events coming up in the next week to your calendar, and make sure to set reminders.

3. Close the Calendar app.

More Apps, More Fun

We've looked at a few of the most popular apps, but many more come with your computer. Therefore, your next challenge is to go exploring! Scroll through the full apps list of the apps on the left side of the Start menu and check out a few of these apps:

* **News:** Keep up-to-date with the latest news in your region.

* **People:** This is a digital address book to help you keep track of people you know and their contact details.

* **Sports:** Find out the latest sports news and scores.

* **Voice Recorder:** Record yourself talking using your microphone. This app is great for taking quick notes or recording messages to send to someone.

Don't be afraid to try out any of the other apps you find. As mentioned at the beginning of this lesson, you won't be able to accidentally spend any money, so there's no risk. Do keep in mind, though, that some apps (such as News and Sports) require you to be connected to the internet to work properly.

Phew, We Did It!

In this lesson, we looked at using some of the free, built-in apps that come with your computer. You learned to do the following:

* Play card games using the Microsoft Solitaire Collection

* Check the weather using the Weather app

* Add events to your calendar

In the next lesson, you'll start looking at putting photos on your computer.

LESSON REVIEW

Congratulations! You've completed Lesson 2. The following activities will help you review what you learned. If you can complete all of these activities with confidence, then you are ready for Lesson 3. If not, don't lose heart—just keep practicing by trying out different apps!

1. Open Microsoft Solitaire Collection and win a game of FreeCell.

2. Open the Weather app and check tomorrow's maximum temperature in your hometown.

3. Open the Calendar and add an event titled "Complete Lesson 3" for some time during the next week. Be sure to allocate at least two hours!

4. Explore the apps in the Start menu and try out any apps you like the look of.

LESSON 3
THE PHOTOS
APP

This lesson covers the Photos app and shows you
a simple and useful way to enjoy your photos.

The Photos app is another free app that will already be on your Windows 10 computer. We'll begin by exploring how to add photos to your computer from a camera or phone, and then you'll see how to view and edit your images. We'll finish this lesson with printing your photos so you can share them with friends or put them in a frame!

Why Should I Use the Photos App?

The Photos app makes it easy to manage your digital photos. Digital photos are found everywhere in modern life—and for good reason! Unlike with traditional photo albums, you can store hundreds, even thousands of photos in an orderly and easily managed fashion, without taking up space in your home. Digital photos mean there's no waste, and because you're not using film, you can take as many photos as will fit on your camera's or phone's memory—which tends to be thousands! You just take as many photos as you want and then look at the digital files of these photos to decide which ones you want to keep, which to print, and which to delete to free up space for even more photos.

You can also do much more with digital photos than you can with film photographs. With the Photos app, you can improve, fix, and edit your photos; you can rotate photos to the correct orientation; and you can crop photos to remove objects. When you're happy with your photos, you can print as many copies as you like to share with friends and family, or send digital copies for people to receive instantly (we'll look at emailing picture files in Lesson 4).

From Film Photos to Digital Photos

In this lesson, you'll learn to add photos to the Photos app from a digital camera or phone. This is wonderfully easy, but it only works for digital photos, not older hard-copy photos that have been developed using film. However, if you do have a large collection of film photos, there is a way to create a digital version of them to use with the Photos app: you need to scan them with a *scanner*, which is an external device that basically creates a digital copy of the photo. Scanners are quite cheap to buy, and many public libraries will have one. To make things even easier, your computer has a Scan app. To find out more about how to connect a scanner, see "Connecting a Printer, Scanner, Webcam, or Other Device" on page 293.

Another quick way to digitize print photos is simply to take a picture of them using a phone or digital camera. This is an easy way to share older photos with friends and family online, although the quality of the picture may not be high enough to make new prints.

Connecting Your Camera or Phone

If you've taken photos using your computer or tablet's camera, the photos will appear in the Photos app without your needing to add them! In this case, you can skip ahead to "Viewing a Photo" on page 80. But if you've taken photos on your phone or digital camera, you need to add them to your computer before you can work with them in the Photos app.

First, you need to connect your camera or phone to your computer. Most cameras and phones will come with a cable, called a *USB cable*, to allow you to do this. The cable will look something like the one shown in the following figures and will have a small rectangular plug on one end and a larger rectangular plug on the other. Once you've found the cable for your phone or camera, follow these steps:

1. Plug the larger end of the cable into your computer. If you're using a laptop or tablet, find a small rectangular port on the side that fits the cable, as shown below.

 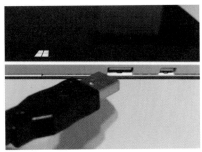

If you're using a desktop computer, the ports will be on the main computer unit. There are usually ports on the front of the unit, but if you can't find them, look on the back of the computer.

2 Plug the smaller end of the cable into your camera or phone, as shown here.

3 Turn the camera or phone on. Most cameras will connect automatically; however, some may require you to press a button on the camera or phone to connect. On an iPhone, for example, you need to press **Trust** before you can access your photos on a separate device. If your camera or phone doesn't seem to be connecting, look at its screen and see if there are any instructions. Check your camera's manual for details.

Importing Photos

It's time to add the photos from your camera or phone to the Photos app! This is called *importing* photos, which just means the photos will be copied from your device and stored on your computer. Before you begin, it's important to know that adding the photos to the Photos app won't delete your photos from the camera. We'll cover how to remove photos from your camera later, since it can be good for freeing up space, but this action won't occur automatically. To import your photos, follow these steps:

1 Click the **start button** in the bottom-left corner of the screen.

2 The Start menu will appear. Find the **Photos** tile, highlighted next, and click it once.

3 If you don't see this tile in the Start menu, click in the search box next to the start button and then type **photos**. Click **Photos** from the list that appears.

4 This should bring up the Photos app. Your screen might look a little different, depending on which version of the Photos app you have.

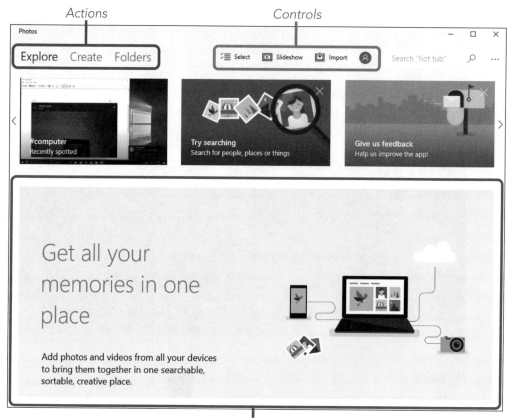

Actions

Controls

This is where your photos will appear.

5 The **Import** button loads pictures from your camera or phone into your computer to use in the Photos app. Click this button now.

6 If you have more than one camera, phone, or other photo device connected, you'll be asked which device to import from. Choose the device you just connected with the cable by clicking it once. If you only have one device connected, the app will know to import from that device, and you won't see this step.

7 If you receive a message stating "There's nothing to import" or if your device doesn't appear in the list, double-check your phone or camera's screen to see if there's a button labeled **Trust** or **Allow**.

If there is, press it to let your computer see your photos. Otherwise, double-check the cable connection between the computer and your device.

8 Once you've chosen a device, you should see a list of the photos stored on that device. These photos appear small so they can be listed efficiently, but once they are imported, you can view them much bigger! You will see a check mark next to the photos that are going to be imported, as shown in the following figure. The app will assume you want every photo imported unless you tell it otherwise by *deselecting* photos. If you don't want certain photos to be imported, just click once on the photo, and the check mark will disappear, meaning it will not be imported.

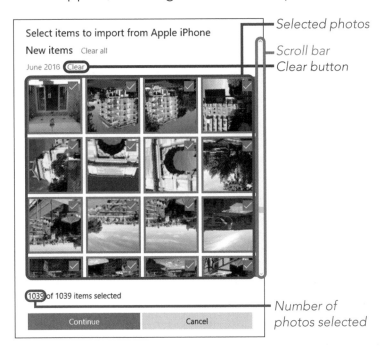

Let's have a closer look at what you're seeing on the screen:

* **Selected photos:** Small versions of the photos appear in a list, and the photos selected for import are shown with a checkmark. If you don't want to important a certain photo, click it once, and the checkmark should disappear.

✳ **Number of photos selected:** This is the number of photos on your device selected for import. It might be higher than you realized!

✳ **Clear:** If you only want to import a few photos but lots of photos are selected, click the **Clear** button once to deselect all the photos for a particular month, and then scroll through and click any photos you do want to import. Using the Clear button can be much quicker than deselecting all the photos one by one!

✳ **Scroll bar:** If there are lots of photos on your device, you'll need to scroll down to see the rest of them. To do this, click the scroll bar and hold the mouse button down; then drag the mouse down and up, like you did in Lesson 1. This will move the screen of the Photos app to reveal more photos.

9 When you're happy with the photos selected for import, click the **Continue** button, shown in the previous figure.

10 A window like the one shown next will appear, asking you to confirm that you want to import the photos. If you want to delete the photos from the device once they've been imported, click the checkbox labeled **Delete imported items from [your device] after importing**.

Start importing?

You selected 8 photos, which will be imported to this folder:

C:\Users\ceewi_gj5nqzl\Pictures
Change where they're imported

Import into folders organised by

Month

☐ Delete imported items from Apple iPhone after importing

Import   Cancel

Once they've been deleted, they'll be gone for good from your device. They will, however, be stored on your computer at that point. This can be a good idea if you're running out of space for more photos on your device.

11 Click the **Import** button.

12 The photos will now begin importing. Depending on how many photos there are, this might take a minute or two. You can see the progress at the top of the screen. Once this bar fills, the import is done.

13 When the import is complete, your photos will be grouped by the date they were taken, as shown here. You may need to scroll down the page with the scroll bar to see all of your photos.

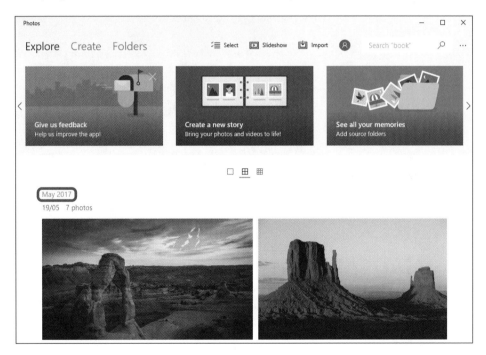

Congratulations—you've imported your photos!

ACTIVITY #5

In this activity, you'll take and import a few photos using your camera or phone to view or edit later.

1. Take the following photos with your camera:

    *   A landscape photo with an object, like a plant, in the middle

    *   An upside-down photo of a tree

    *   A dark corner of your garden or a room

    *   A few more photos of your house or garden

2. Connect your camera or phone to your computer using its cable.

3. Import your new photos into the Photos app, but don't delete the photos from the camera. Remember, if you want to add just a few photos, it might be best to click the **Clear** button and then select those few photos to import.

Viewing a Photo

Now that you have some photos in your Photo app, it's time to enjoy them! To view a photo, follow these steps:

1 Click the photo you want to view.

2   This should display the photo on its own in a larger size. Remember from Lesson 1 that you can make the app take up the full screen by clicking the **maximize button** at the top right (highlighted next). This lets you see your photo at an even bigger size. You can also zoom in on your photo by double-clicking it—that is, by clicking the left mouse button twice in quick succession.

3   You can return to the list of photos by clicking the **back button** at the top-left corner of the screen (on a tablet, this arrow will appear at the bottom-left corner).

Deleting Unwanted Photos

Now that you've viewed your photos, you may decide that you don't want to keep some of them (if you don't like them, for example, or if you have lots of photos of the same thing and just want to keep the best ones). Fortunately, the Photos app lets you delete photos easily. To delete a photo, follow these steps:

1   Find the photo you want to delete and click it to view it at full size.

2   Click the **delete button** at the top of the screen (highlighted here).

3   A box will appear to confirm that you're certain you want to delete the photo. Click **Delete**.

ACTIVITY #6

In this activity, you're going to delete a photo you took of your garden or room in Activity #5.

1.   View the photos you took in Activity #5 and find the ones of your garden or room.

2.   Delete the one you like least.

Let's Get Editing!

We've all taken a less-than-perfect photo before! Maybe you took the photo upside down or accidently included your thumb or some other unwanted item in the shot. All is not lost. The Photos app can help you fix and improve your photo! Try it out:

1 Find the photo you want to edit and click it to view it at full size.

2 Click the **Edit & Create** button at the top of the screen.

3 A drop-down menu will appear. Click the **Edit** button.

4 This should open a list of editing options in columns along the right side of the screen, as shown here.

CROP AND ROTATE

This tool lets you remove unwanted parts of a photo and rotate photos.

1 Click **Crop and rotate** to bring up a Crop and Rotate screen.

2 A box with four white dots should appear around the image. Click a dot and drag it inward to select the area of the photo you want to keep. The area outside of the box will be cropped out.

3 Click the **Rotate** button to rotate the picture clockwise by 90°.

4 Once you're happy with the cropping and rotation, click **Done** at the bottom of the screen to go back to the editing screen.

IMPROVE QUALITY WITH ENHANCE

The Enhance tool automatically adjusts a photo using some default settings to try to fix aspects such as lighting and color by boosting contrast and saturation where needed.

1 Click **Enhance your photo**.

2 A white slider will appear over the "Enhance your photo" button. Click and drag the slider left or right to decrease or increase the enhancement effect until you like what you see.

ADDING EFFECTS WITH FILTERS

Filters change the shades or colors of your photo for dramatic effect. Using filters is a popular way to edit your photos. The name of each filter appears beneath a small preview version of your photo, which shows you how the photo may appear with that filter applied.

1 Click a filter (the preview image of your photo, not the name) to apply it.

2 A white slider should appear below the image. Drag the slider left or right to decrease or increase the filter effect.

FURTHER ADJUSTMENTS

There are a few more adjustments you can use to change the light, color, or clarity of your image.

1 Click the **Adjust** tab.

2 The following adjustment options should appear:

  * **Light:** Makes the photo as a whole lighter or darker.

  * **Color:** Increases or decreases the color saturation, which makes the colors more or less vibrant, respectively.

  * **Clarity:** Makes the image sharper (less blurred) or softer (more blurred).

  * **Vignette:** Darkens the edges of the image.

  * **Red Eye:** Removes the "red eye" effect from faces.

  * **Spot Fix:** Fixes blemishes or other small imperfections in the image.

3 Click an adjustment to apply it and drag the white slider from left to right to change the amount of the adjustment.

SAVING YOUR EDITS

Once you've finished editing your photo, you'll want to save your hard-earned improvements!

1 Find the **Save** button at the bottom of the editing screen and click it. Your edited photo will now be saved!

2 If you decide you don't like your edits and would prefer to have your original photo back, click **Undo all**. This will remove all of your edits.

Printing Old-Fashioned Hard Copies

After you've edited your photos into masterpieces, you might want to print them to put in a picture frame or to show your friends! For best results when printing important images, it's a good idea to use photo paper, which you can buy from any office supply store. Photo paper costs a bit more than ordinary paper but gives you much better-looking photos.

> *** NOTE:** *To print a photo, your computer must be connected to a printer. See "Connecting a Printer, Scanner, Webcam, or Other Device" on page 293 for instructions on setting up your computer with a printer.*

To print a photo, follow these steps:

1   Find a photo you want to print, and click it to view it at full size. If you want to make any edits, do so now before you print.

2   Click the **print button** in the control section about the photo, like in the image shown next.

3   This will open a window with a preview of the printout on the right side and some printing options on the left side. Let's take a look at some of the important options:

   *   **Printer:** Make sure the correct printer is selected using this drop-down box.

> *** TIP:** *Printers are listed in the Photos app by their make and model. If you aren't sure which printer from the list is the one you're connected to, compare the make and the model number to the make and model of your printer. You can usually find this on the top or front of your printer.*

   *   **Copies:** Use the plus button on the right to print more than one copy of your photo.

* **Orientation:** From here you can select whether you want to print in landscape or portrait mode. A landscape image is wider than it is tall; a portrait image is taller than it is wide.

* **Paper size:** It's important to make sure you select the correct paper size; otherwise, your photo probably won't print. Normal plain printing paper is generally letter size, but you can buy 4"×6" photo paper and a variety of other sizes. If you're using photo paper, the size should be listed on the front or back of the packaging.

* **Paper type:** Here you need to choose what kind of paper you're using. If you're using normal copy paper, leave Plain Paper as the setting. If you're using photo paper, it's important to select Photo Paper here.

* **Photo size:** This is how big the photo will be when printed.

* **Fit:** This option changes how the photo is printed if it doesn't exactly match your paper size. If set to **Full Page**, the edges of the photo may be cut off so that it fills the entire page. If set to **Shrink to Fit**, the entire photo will be printed, which may leave some gaps on the sides.

* **Color mode:** This lets you choose whether you want the photo to be printed in color or black and white.

4   After you've chosen your print settings, click the **Print** button.

Your image should now be printed!

Phew, We Did It!

In this lesson, we looked at using the Photos app. We imported pictures from a camera and discussed how to edit the photos and print them. In this lesson, you learned to do the following:

* Connect a camera or phone to your computer

* Import photos from your camera or phone

* View and delete photos on your computer

* Make alterations to your photos, including cropping, rotating, and enhancing

* Print your photos

In the next lesson, you'll learn to send and receive emails from your computer.

LESSON REVIEW

Congratulations! You've completed Lesson 3. Take this opportunity to review what you've learned by completing the following activities. If you can complete all of these activities with confidence, you're ready for Lesson 4. If not, just keep practicing by importing, viewing, and editing photos!

1. Take some photos with your camera or phone. Try to take some poor-quality photos so you can practice editing and adjusting them.

2. Connect your camera to your computer.

3. Import those photos to your computer.

4. Edit the pictures to improve them. Experiment with some of the different editing options.

5. Delete the photos that couldn't be satisfactorily improved by editing.

6. Print your favorite photo.

LESSON 4
EMAIL

In this lesson, you'll learn how to set up
the Windows Mail app, send emails,
receive and reply to emails, and send photos.

What Exactly Is Email?

Email is electronic mail that you can send and receive using your computer. There are many advantages to email: it's free to send and receive regardless of the message length; it's instant; and you can send pictures, videos, links to interesting websites, and much more. Millions of people around the world rely on email for their daily correspondence. And because so many people use email, it's likely that many of your friends and family are already using it, making it a simple way to keep in touch with people you know.

Many apps and email services refer to emails as "messages," so if you see the term *message* instead of *email*, just know that it's often the same thing.

Like with traditional mail, to send an email you need to know *where* to send it. This is where email addresses come in: an *email address* is a unique address that ensures your email goes precisely to the right person. This also means that people can contact you at your email address without worrying that their email has gone to the wrong person. An email address might look like this: *chrisewin@outlook.com.*

All email addresses have an @ symbol (pronounced "at") in the middle. The part before the @ symbol is your unique address name, which you choose when setting up your email account. The part after the @ symbol is the email provider you're using. For example, Google email addresses end in *@gmail.com,* and Microsoft email addresses end in *@outlook.com.*

You will need to use either a Microsoft account or your own email address to follow along with the chapter. If you followed the steps in "Setting Up Your Computer" on page 17, you'll already have a Microsoft account with an email address that ends in *@outlook.com.* If not, consult "Switching to a Microsoft Account" on page 297 to check whether you have a Microsoft account and then set one up if you do not.

Opening the Mail App

Windows 10 includes the built-in Mail app, which makes sending and receiving emails easier. If you've used an older Windows computer, you may be familiar with Windows Live Mail or Outlook Express, which are also email programs. The Mail app performs a similar function, but its layout is quite different from Live Mail and Outlook Express. There are other ways to use email with web-based email managers such as Gmail and Hotmail, but to keep things simple, we'll focus on the Mail app.

To open the Mail app, follow these steps:

1   Click the **start button** in the bottom-left corner of the screen.

2   The Start menu will appear. Find the **Mail** tile, shown next, and click it once. If you can't find the Mail tile, click in the search box next to the start button, type **mail**, and click **Mail** from the list that appears.

The Mail app will open.

Setting Up the Mail App

If this is your first time using the Mail app, you'll be asked to go through a quick setup process. This involves adding your email address to the Mail app so you can send and receive messages.

1 Click the **Get started** button, shown here.

2 If the *@outlook.com* email account you created in "Setting Up Your Computer" on page 17 is the only email address you want to use, click **Ready to go** and then skip ahead to "Checking Your Email" on page 96. If you'd like to set up additional accounts, continue to step 3.

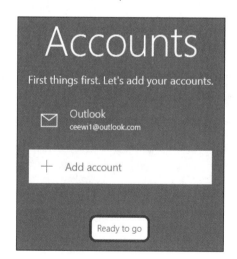

3   You can use Mail to manage all of your email accounts. To add a second email account, click the **Add account** button.

4   You'll be asked to choose the type of account you want to add from a list of email providers. You can tell what email provider you have from your email address. If it ends in *@yahoo.com*, for example, Yahoo is your provider, and you have a Yahoo email account. Here are some other popular account types:

  ∗   **Outlook.com:** An address using this type of account ends in *@outlook.com* or *@hotmail.com*.

  ∗   **Google:** A Google email address ends in *@gmail.com*.

  ∗   **iCloud (Apple):** An address using this type of account ends in *@iCloud.com*.

5   Select your email provider from the list. (If your email provider isn't listed, select **Other account**.) Different email providers will ask for slightly different information. Enter the information requested by your provider.

6   Click **Done** to confirm your account has been set up, as shown next.

All done!
Your account was set up successfully.

✉ ceewi1@gmail.com

Done

7   Click the **Ready to go** button.

Congratulations! Your email is ready to use.

Checking Your Email

After you've set up your email account, the Mail app should open. The screen is divided into three sections:

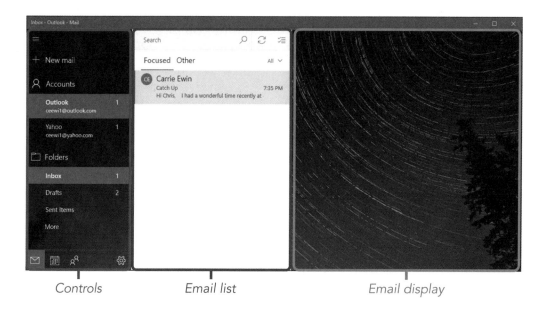

Controls   Email list   Email display

* **Controls:** This area has tools for creating a new email mesesage, switching accounts, selecting various folders, and so on.

* **Email list:** The middle section shows a list of the emails in the selected folder—for example, the Inbox or Sent Items folder.

* **Email display area:** When you select a message in the email list, the contents of the message will be displayed on the right. If no message is selected, you'll see a background image instead.

RECEIVING AN EMAIL

All the emails you receive appear in your Inbox. When your Inbox is selected, the messages will be displayed in a list in the middle of the screen. Each message in the email list contains five main pieces of information, as shown in the following figure.

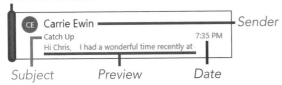

Unread indicator

Carrie Ewin — Sender

Catch Up — 7:35 PM

Hi Chris, I had a wonderful time recently at

Subject   Preview   Date

* **Unread:** A vertical blue strip along the left side of the message means you haven't read the message.

* **Sender:** This is the name of the person who sent the email.

* **Subject:** This blue text describes what the email is about; this is written by the sender.

* **Preview:** This shows the first few words of the email.

* **Date:** Next to the preview is the date the email was sent. If the email was sent recently, you'll see the time it was sent.

* **NOTE:** *Some, but not all, email accounts will separate your Inbox into two sections labeled **Focused** and **Other**. Focused messages are ones that Microsoft thinks you're most likely to want to read, while Other messages contain all the rest. If your account separates messages like this, you'll start off by seeing Focused messages, but you can click the Other heading to see the rest.*

ACTIVITY #7

In this activity, you'll use an email from your Inbox to answer the following questions:

* Have you read the email before?

* Who sent you the email?

* When was the email sent?

OPENING AN EMAIL

Clicking an email to view its contents is called *opening* an email, like opening a letter. Using the email you looked at in Activity #7, follow these steps:

1   Click once on the email you want to read, listed in the Inbox.

2   The contents of that email will now be displayed on the right.

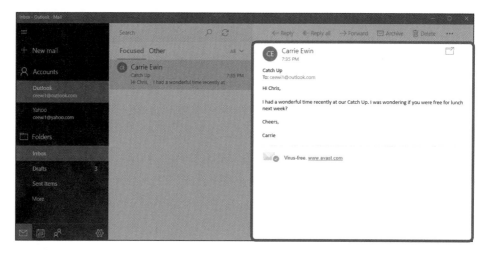

READING AN EMAIL

Some emails, like the one shown next, are too long to fit on the screen. Fortunately, you can use a *scroll bar* on the right side of the screen to see the rest of the message. You can click the arrow at the bottom of the scroll bar to move down the email, and the arrow at the top takes you back up. If you have a mouse with a scroll wheel, you can roll your scroll wheel up or down to do the same.

At the top of an email, you should see who sent the email and when, with the subject of the email underneath. Below that, the email lists the recipients (emails can be sent to multiple people at once, so you might not be the only recipient). Then the message of the email will follow.

Sender   *Date and time it was sent*   *Scroll bar*

The topic and intent of an email vary depending on the sender. Friends and family use email to keep in touch, but companies can also send emails advertising their products or services. There isn't necessarily anything wrong with that. After all, you might like to receive a special offer from your local store once in a while. But companies should give you the ability to opt out of, or "unsubscribe" from, their emails if you don't want to receive their ads. Just click the link in the email that reads "Unsubscribe." It often appears at the bottom of the email. The exact wording varies, but you should be able to find the link in each email.

SWITCHING TO ANOTHER EMAIL ACCOUNT

If you've set up a second email address in the Mail app, you'll need to switch to that account before you can read its emails. You should see your accounts listed on the left side of the screen. The number beside an account tells you how many unread emails that account currently has. To switch to another account, simply click the one you want to switch to, as shown next.

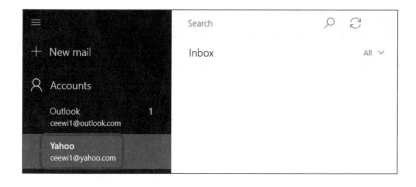

When you switch to another account, your screen should remain the same, but you'll be viewing the list of emails sent to that email address.

Sending an Email

Now that you know how to read emails, it's time to send one of your own. Remember, you can send an email to anybody in the world for free—as long as you know their correct email address. To send an email message, follow these steps:

1. From the controls on the left side of the screen, click the **New mail** button, highlighted here.

2. The new mail screen, which should look like the following image, will appear on the right side of the screen.

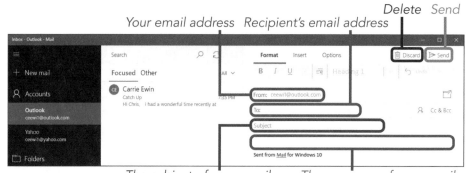

Your email address   Recipient's email address   Delete   Send

The subject of your email   The message of your email

3 Click in the **To** box and type the email address of the person you want to send your message to. It is very important that you type their email address correctly. If you make a typo, click at the end of the email address to place your cursor there and then use the BACKSPACE key to delete your mistake. Now try again!

The good news is that Mail remembers the addresses of people you've sent emails to in the past. If you start typing their address again, the complete address should show up underneath, as shown next, and you can click the address to fill it in automatically.

4 Click in the **Subject** box to place your cursor there and then type a few words that describe your email. The word "Subject" will be there at first but disappear as soon as you start typing.

5 Click the larger box below the Subject to place your cursor there and then type your email message.

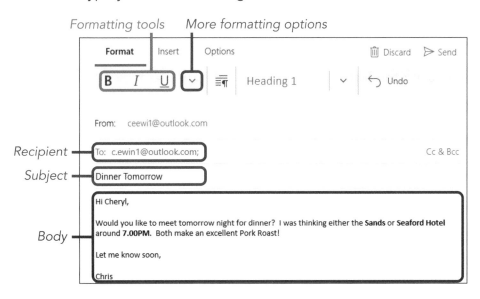

Note that the message area might already contain the text "Sent from Mail for Windows 10." You can delete this text or just type your message above it. You can also *format* the text in your email with bold text and other options. To learn more about formatting, flip forward to Lesson 12—the formatting tools in WordPad are very similar to the ones in Mail.

6   When you're ready to send the message, click the **Send** button in the top-right corner. If you decide not to send the message, click the **Discard** button to delete the message you've just typed and go back to your Inbox.

Replying to an Email

The best way to respond to an email you've received is by sending a *reply*. When you click the Reply button, Mail creates an email with the address of the original sender already filled in. The Subject box keeps the subject used in the original email sent to you but with "RE:" before it to indicate that it's a reply. This saves you a lot of work and makes replying easy!

The contents of the original email should be included below your new message to remind everyone what's being discussed. To reply to an email, follow these steps:

1   Click an email to open it, like you did earlier.

2   Click the **Reply** button at the top of the email display area.

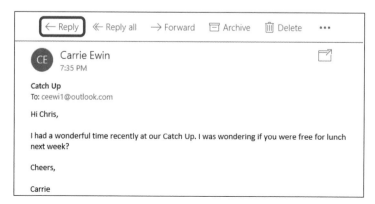

✱ NOTE: *If there is more than one recipient in an email, you can click* **Reply all** *instead of Reply to send your reply to everyone on the recipient list. You can also click* **Forward** *if you want to pass the email on to somebody else.*

3 A reply email will open, with a blank area where you can type your response. Notice that the To box and Subject box are filled in and the original message is included below the blank area. Your cursor should be blinking in the space above the original message.

4 Type your reply. When you're ready, click the **Send** button in the top-right corner of the message.

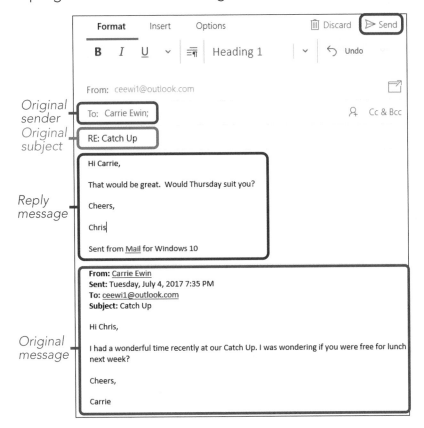

You can reply to a reply, too. This will create an *email chain,* or *thread,* that can go on indefinitely. But if you're writing about something new, it's better to start a new email chain. This makes it easier to manage your emails and find the exact email you're looking for.

ACTIVITY #8

In this activity, you'll practice sending and replying to emails.

1. Send an email to a friend asking them to reply—you can let them know you're doing an exercise if you want!

2. When you get a reply, read their message.

3. Send a reply back to their message.

Sending Pictures and Other Files

Another great thing about email is that you can send electronic files such as photos or a résumé, and your recipient gets them almost instantly. An electronic file that's added to an email is called an *attachment*. It's the modern equivalent of attaching a photo to a letter with a paper clip! To add an attachment to a new email, follow these steps:

1 From the controls on the left side of the screen, click the **New mail** button to create a new email.

2 Write an email, just as you did earlier, by typing the other person's email address, a subject, and a brief message.

3 Click the **Insert** button at the top of the screen. A small menu will appear that shows the different things you can insert.

4 From this list, click the **Files** button, highlighted next.

5 This should bring up a screen asking you to choose the files you want to send. Find the *Pictures* folder on the left side of the screen, highlighted here.

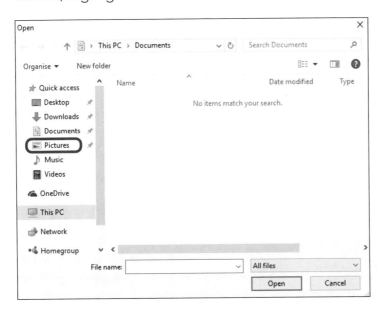

✳ **NOTE:** *Files on your computer are organized and stored in folders. We'll look more at storing and finding files in Lesson 13. For now, we'll focus on attaching pictures, but you can use this exact same process to attach all sorts of files too.*

6 Click the *Pictures* folder once to open it. If you can't see the folder, you might need to scroll through the options. You can scroll by clicking the scroll bar and, while holding down the mouse button, dragging the mouse up or down to move the bar.

7 The screen should now show the contents of the *Pictures* folder. It might contain a number of other folders, represented by icons that look like manila folders (shown next). This helps organize your photos so you can easily find them. If you've completed Lesson 3, you should find the pictures you imported in a folder labeled with the year and month you imported them.

8 Double-click the folder containing your Lesson 3 photos, labeled with the year and month you imported them, as shown here.

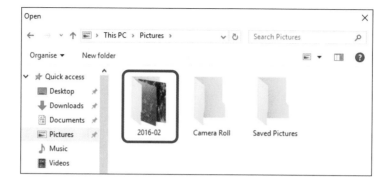

9 This opens that folder to show its contents. Find and click the picture you want to attach to your email; then click the **Open** button, as shown here.

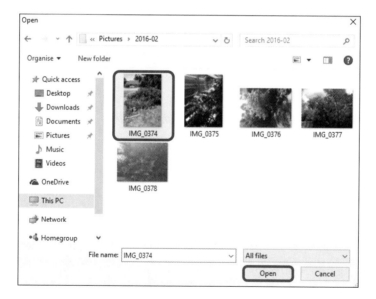

10 You should now see a smaller version of your attached picture above your message, as shown next.

✱ **NOTE:** *If you accidentally attach the wrong file and want to remove it, you can do so by clicking the* **close button** *in the top-right corner of the attachment.*

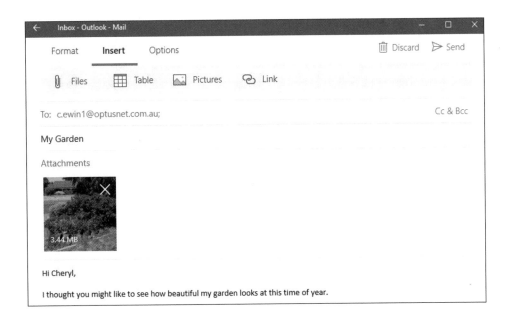

11 To add more than one file, follow these steps again, starting with step 4. You have a limit on the number of files you can add to one email. If Mail says you've exceeded that limit, you might need to send more than one email to accommodate all of your pictures.

12 Click the **Send** button to send your email with the attached photo.

ACTIVITY #9

In this activity, you're going to attach a photo to an email.

1. Compose an email with a message to a friend or family member.

2. Attach a photo relevant to the message or one you think they'd like.

3. Send your email with your attached photo.

Opening Attachments

Just as you can send attachments to your friends, your friends can send attachments (such as photos) to you. If you receive an email with an attachment, it will have an image of a paper clip in the top-right corner, making it easy to recognize in your Inbox. You need to open the email to see the attachment.

1 Look at your Inbox and find an email with a paper clip icon, indicating that it contains an attachment.

2 Click the email to display the message.

3 The attachment should be shown above the message, just like when you added an attachment to an email earlier. It should be a small symbol surrounded by a light gray box, like in the following figure. Click once on the attachment.

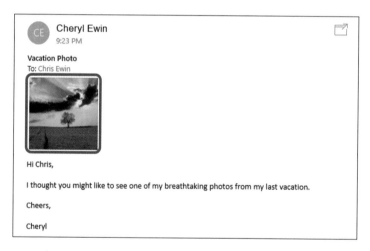

✳ WARNING: *Be aware that attachments from unknown sources can contain viruses designed to harm your computer. You should never open an attachment unless you trust the person who sent it. For more tips about email security, skip to Lesson 14.*

4 The attachment opens in a separate window, as shown next. To return to your Inbox, click the **close button**.

Deleting an Email

It's always a good idea to delete unwanted emails, making it easier to find the emails you *do* need. To delete an email, follow these steps:

1 Click the unwanted email in the list of messages.

2 Click the **Delete** button in the top-right corner of the message display, as shown next.

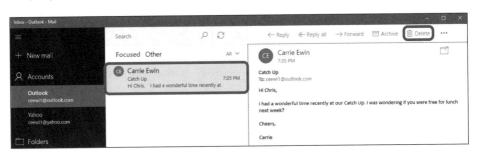

3 A red bar should appear at the bottom of the screen to let you know that the email has been deleted. If you delete the wrong email or decide you didn't want to delete the email after all, you can click the **Undo** button to bring it back. This bar will disappear after a little while, so you need to be fairly quick if you want to bring the email back in this way.

ACTIVITY #10

In this activity, you'll practice opening an attachment that a friend has sent you.

1. Find an email with an attachment in your Inbox. If you don't have an email with an attachment, ask a friend to send you one.

2. Open the email and then open the attachment.

3. Close the attachment.

4. Delete the email.

Searching for Emails

If you keep a lot of emails in your Inbox, it can be difficult to find a particular one you want to read. Fortunately, the Mail app lets you search for emails. You can search for the person who sent the email, the subject line, or even particular words within the message. To search for an email, follow these steps:

1 Click the **Search** box at the top of the screen, highlighted next.

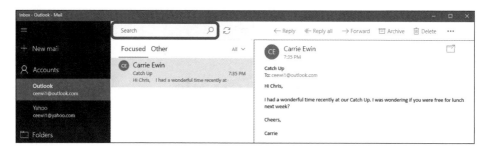

2 Type the words you want to search for, such as the sender's name or email address, the subject of the email, or particular words that you remember from the email. Then press the ENTER key.

3 A list of results should appear. Words that you searched for will be highlighted in yellow. Click the message you want to read to display it on the right side of the screen.

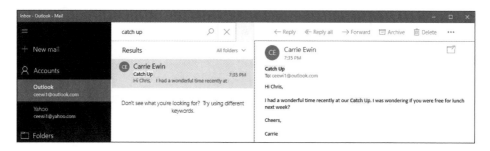

4 When you're done searching, you can click the **close button** next to the search box (shown next) to go back to the Inbox.

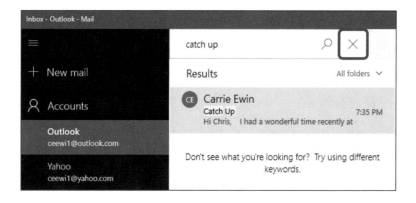

You should now see the Inbox again.

Staying Safe with Emails

While email is a convenient way to keep in touch with your friends and family members, scammers might use emails to try to trick you into giving them your financial details or into installing a virus on your computer. They might attempt this by pretending to be a bank or a legitimate company, asking you to click a link or provide personal information. However, a real bank would *never* ask for information via email. If you're concerned that an email from a bank might be a scam, contact the bank directly (not using the contact details provided in the email) to confirm. For more information about staying safe with emails, jump forward to Lesson 14.

Phew, We Did It!

In this lesson, we looked at using the Mail app to set up and organize emails. You learned to do the following:

✳ Set up the Mail app

✳ Add other email accounts

✳ Read, send, and reply to emails

✳ Send pictures and files, and open attachments from other people

* Delete emails

* Search for emails

In the next lesson, you'll learn to browse websites and explore the internet.

LESSON REVIEW

Congratulations, you've completed Lesson 4. Take this opportunity to review what you've learned by completing the following tasks. If you can complete all of these tasks with confidence, you're ready for Lesson 5. If not, just keep practicing by sending more emails and replying to those you receive!

1. Open the **Mail** app.

2. Compose an email to a friend.

3. Ask your friend to send you an email in reply.

4. Read the message your friend has sent you.

5. Reply to the email. Include an attachment in your reply.

6. Delete your friend's email.

LESSON 5
INTRODUCING THE INTERNET

Let's get on the internet!

The internet is like a giant web of computers that talk to each other and exchange information. The internet offers you endless resources for finding information, communicating with friends and family, and entertaining yourself. Here's a taste of some exciting things you can do on the internet:

* Read the latest news and check the weather

* Look up local information such as movie times, operating hours for shops and restaurants, and bus schedules

* Get walking, driving, or public transportation directions

* Read articles about technology, gardening, and more

* Watch helpful videos, how-to guides, or even movies and TV shows

The internet is huge, so this lesson just covers the basics of accessing a website and finding your way around, as well as printing from the internet and saving shortcuts to your favorite websites. Over the course of this book, you'll learn much more about using the internet. Before you can start using the internet, though, you need be connected to it via an internet service provider (ISP) such as AT&T or Comcast. Flip back to "Setting Up an Internet Connection" on page 17 to find out more about getting connected.

Opening Microsoft Edge

We're going to access the internet with a *web browser*, which is a special app that lets you open and view the different websites on the internet. Many different browsers are available, like Internet Explorer and Google Chrome. By and large, they all do the same thing—enable you to browse the internet! We'll use Microsoft's newest browser, *Microsoft Edge*, because it comes included on all Windows 10 computers.

Let's begin by opening Microsoft Edge:

1 Click the **Microsoft Edge** button from the taskbar.

> **✳ NOTE:** *If you can't see the Microsoft Edge icon in the taskbar, you can also open the app by clicking the **start button** and then clicking the **Microsoft Edge** tile.*

2 The first time you open Microsoft Edge, you might see a setup screen similar to the one shown here. This welcome screen lets you customize your Microsoft Edge web browser, but you don't need to worry about it right now. If you do see this screen, simply close Microsoft Edge using the close button.

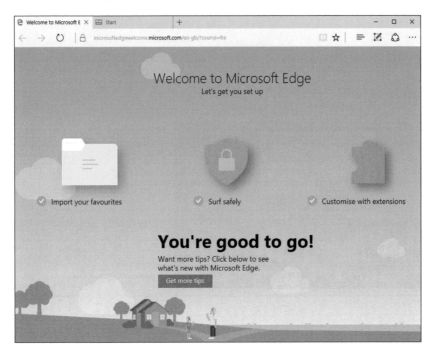

3 When you click the close button, you'll be asked if you want to close all tabs. We'll look at tabs in more detail in "Using Tabs" on page 126, but for now click the **Close all** button, highlighted next.

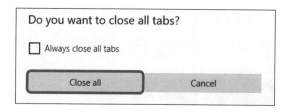

4   Now that you've seen this initial welcome message, reopen Microsoft Edge.

This time, you'll be taken to your *home page*. Your home page is simply the first page you see when you access the internet. A lot of internet browsers offer built-in home pages with helpful and interesting information, such as pages you've visited recently. Microsoft Edge has a particularly useful home page, shown here, that's called the *Start page*.

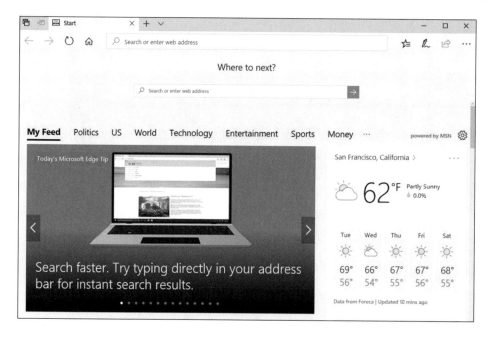

This page suggests content it thinks you'll find interesting, such as your local news and weather. You can click any of the articles to read more about them. For now, though, we'll focus on the bar at the top of the screen, highlighted next. This is the *address bar*, which has the text "Search or enter web address."

If you have an older version of Microsoft Edge, you might see this bar underneath a *Where to next?* heading. The address bar is one of the most important parts of the Microsoft Edge browser because it lets you search for any site or page on the internet.

What Is a Website?

The internet hosts a huge number of different *websites* (or just *sites* for short) run by different companies, organizations, or individuals. For example, Walmart, Best Buy, and the *New York Times* all operate their own websites, and each has a different purpose and different content. Most sites break down their content into a number of *pages* to make it easier to read and organize. For example, a news site like the *New York Times* might devote one page to each news article it covers, whereas a store such as Walmart or Best Buy might have a page for each product it sells. This collection of sites makes up the *World Wide Web*, or *the web* for short. To begin exploring the web, we need a way to navigate to the sites. One way to do that is to use a site's unique address.

You might have seen various companies advertise their websites with addresses like *www.bestbuy.com* or *www.gumtree.com.au*. A web address gives you an easy way to find a particular site by letting you go straight there, like with a street address. As you'll see in Lesson 6, you can also search for a site without using its web address, but using its address is often quicker and ensures you're going to the right site.

But what do these web addresses actually mean? Let's learn about the parts of a web address, using *www.gumtree.com.au* as an example:

* **www:** This stands for *World Wide Web*. Using *www* is customary in web addresses, but you can usually omit this and the period that comes directly after it when entering a web address in the address bar (for example, *gumtree.com.au*).

* **.gumtree:** This is the unique name of the site. Be sure to type this correctly, as any typos can send you to the wrong site! Web addresses never have spaces, and capitalization doesn't matter.

* **.com:** This part is intended to describe what kind of site it is. For example, *.com* stands for *commercial* and is intended to be used by businesses. You might also see a site ending in *.org*, such as *www.wikipedia.org*, indicating that it's run by an organization (usually a nonprofit). There's also *.edu*, indicating an educational institution like *www.harvard.edu*, and *.gov* for a government site like *www.usa.gov*. These are just guidelines, though; there's nothing preventing someone from registering a *.com* site even if they're not part of a company. So you don't need to pay too much attention to this part except to enter it correctly.

* **.au:** You might have noticed that Gumtree's web address, unlike the others we've discussed, has something after *.com*. The *.au* is a country code that stands for *Australia*. Sites outside the United States often have such a code telling you where they're based, either after *.com* or instead of it (for example, *www.kijiji.ca* is a popular classifieds site in Canada).

ACTIVITY #11

Most web addresses are meant to be recognizable and therefore are similar to the name of the company, organization, or person they represent. This way, you can easily guess the address and visit the site. In this activity, you'll practice guessing a company's web address.

The American publishing company that produced this book is called No Starch, and it has a site! Write down what you think its web address might be.

Opening a Site

Once you have the web address for a site you want to visit, it's time to open the site! Follow these steps to open a site using its web address:

1 Click in the address bar.

2 Enter the address of the site you wish to visit. There's no need to erase the words "Search or enter web address," because they disappear as soon as you start typing. As an example, let's use *www.nostarch.com*.

> ✱ **NOTE:** *As you type, a list of search suggestions should appear below the address bar. We'll look at how this works later.*

3 Press ENTER to go to the site. After the site finishes loading, you should see something like this:

This is the No Starch home page! Just like your web browser, each site has its own home page, which is the page that opens when you first visit the site's main address.

Notice that the address bar is still there at the top of the page. If you decide to go to a different site, you can click in the address bar again, as shown next.

The address should turn blue when you click it. This highlights the text, and when you start typing, the highlighted text will be replaced with what you type. (If the address doesn't turn blue for you, just click at the end of the address and press the BACKSPACE key to delete the address before typing a new one.) Don't forget to press the ENTER key after you've typed the address.

ACTIVITY #12

In this activity, try visiting the following popular sites.

1. Use the address bar to go to *www.washingtonpost.com*.

2. Use the address bar to go to *www.nytimes.com*.

3. Use the address bar to go to *www.nostarch.com* again.

Navigating a Site

The internet is *huge*, and to master it, you'll first need to learn how to find your way around the different pages on a site! You can do this using links. Once you have navigated to a site, you can explore the different pages of that site by clicking the links. *Links* are words or pictures on the page that take you to other pages, usually on the same site. Most sites use links to take you from page to page, making it easy to explore the site.

For example, on the main page at *www.nostarch.com*, the various topics such as Art & Design, General Computing, and Hacking & Computer Security are all links to other pages, as are the book titles and cover pictures. When you click one of these links, it takes you to a page dedicated to that book or topic.

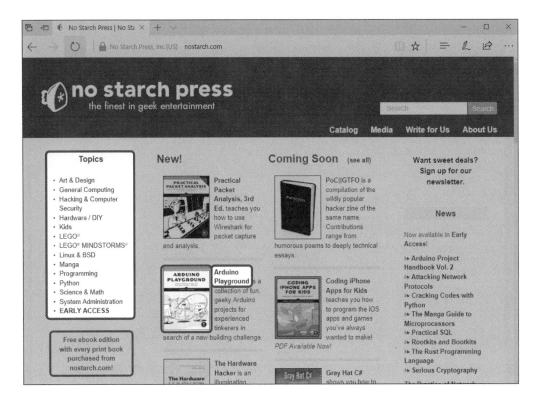

OPENING A LINK

To see the page the link takes you to, you need to open the link. To do this, follow these steps:

1   Find a heading, word, or picture that might be a link and move your mouse pointer over it. The pointer should change to a pointing hand symbol (🖑) if it is indeed a link.

2   Click the link.

The web page that the link points to should now open.

ACTIVITY #13

In this activity, you'll practice using a link to visit a new page.

1.   Go to the No Starch site.

2.   Visit a book's page.

USING THE BACK AND FORWARD BUTTONS

Now that you've visited a page, what's next? If you find another link on that page that you want to see, you can click it just like before. Sometimes, though, you'll want to go back to the page you came from. For example, on the *www.nostarch.com* site, once you're done reading about a specific book, you might want to return to the main page and look at a different book. Fortunately, this is easy to do!

To go back to the previous page, simply click the **back button**. Each time you click the back button, you'll go back one page. Once you reach the Start page, you can't go back any further.

Back Forward

If you accidentally click the back button too many times and end up going back further than you intended, click the **forward button** to go forward again.

ACTIVITY #14

In this activity, you'll practice using the back and forward buttons.

1. Visit the page of one of the books on the No Starch site and then click the back button to go back to the main *www.nostarch.com* page.

2. Click the **forward button** to return to the book you were just looking at.

ZOOMING IN AND OUT

You may find that the words on a web page are too small and difficult to read. This can be a particular problem when using a tablet or laptop, which has a smaller screen. Fortunately, you can zoom in to see a page more clearly by following these steps:

1. Click the **more actions button** in the top-right corner of the page. This button, highlighted next, appears as three small dots.

2   A menu with a few different options should appear. Find the **Zoom** option and click the **+ button** to zoom in to enlarge the page.

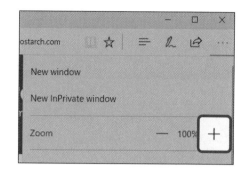

3   You can click the button several times to zoom in even further.

4   Click the **– button** to zoom out and reduce the size of the page.

5   Once you're happy with the size of the text, you can click anywhere else on the page to dismiss the more actions menu.

ACTIVITY #15

In this activity, you'll practice zooming in and out on a site.

1.   Use the **– button** (zoom out) to adjust the site to 75%.

2.   Use the **+ button** (zoom in) to readjust the site to 100%.

Using Tabs

Tabs allow you to have more than one web page open at once in your internet browser. These are named after old-fashioned folders that were organized and labeled using paper tabs. The advantage of tabs in your browser is that you can quickly switch between different sites.

Sometimes, tabs can be tricky to use. You may find that when you click a link or inadvertently click an advertisement, the page or ad opens in a new tab when you didn't mean it to. For example, if you were visiting *www.nytimes.com* and clicked the ad for a digital subscription, a new tab might open, as shown next.

You can see that the back button is grayed out and unusable because a new tab has opened. Above the address bar are two tabs, each referring to the *New York Times*. The tab on the left is the main page for the *New York Times* that we had originally opened, and the one on the right is the new tab that opened for the digital subscription ad.

To close the new tab, simply click the close button on the right side of the tab. Be careful not to click the plus sign (+) next to it, though! That would create yet another new tab that you'd need to close.

GETTING RID OF UNEXPECTED ADS

On some sites, you may see a pop-up ad offering you a free membership, as shown next, or some other ad. These ads can cover most of the screen, making it impossible to read the article underneath. This is an unfortunate side effect of being online; you'll often get unwanted ads popping up. Look for a close button and click it to make the ad go away. Sometimes a timer may appear, and you have to wait five or so seconds before you can close the ad! Unfortunately, you won't be able to close off all ads. The smaller ads that often appear at the top or on the side of a page usually can't be closed.

Printing a Page

Having all this information on the internet is fantastic, but sometimes you'll want a printed copy of the web page. Maybe you've found a great recipe or a discount coupon you'd like to use, or maybe you want to print directions that someone sent you in an email. To print a page, you'll first need to make sure your computer is connected to a printer. See "Connecting a Printer, Scanner, Webcam, or Other Device" on page 293 if you need help setting up your computer with a printer.

To print a page, follow these steps:

1   Open the web page you would like to print.

2   Click the **more actions button**, highlighted next, in the top-right corner of the page.

3   This should bring up the same menu you used to zoom in and out.

4   From the menu, click the **Print** button.

5   You'll see a preview of how the page would look in print. Make sure your printer is selected underneath the Printer heading. If the correct printer is not selected, click the **drop-down arrow** next to the printer name and choose your desired printer from the list. You can change the other options here (see Lesson 3 if you need a reminder of what these options mean), but the default options should be okay to use.

6   Click the **Print** button in the bottom-left corner to print the page.

The web page should now be printed!

Making Shortcuts with Favorites

Now that you know how to start finding your way around the internet, you'll quickly find yourself exploring many interesting sites. When you find a site you like and plan to revisit, you'll want a way to keep track of it. Writing a list on a piece of paper next to your computer is one option, but not a very efficient one. Fortunately, Microsoft Edge provides a handy tool for storing and returning to your favorite sites, helpfully called *favorites*. Once you've added a site to your list of favorites, you can return to it with just a few clicks.

ADDING SITES TO YOUR FAVORITES

To add a web page to your list of favorites, follow these steps:

1   Open the web page that you would like to add to your favorites.

2   After the site loads, click the **add to favorites button**. This appears as a small star, as shown here.

3 A menu will appear with options for creating your new favorite. Make sure that **Favorites** (rather than Reading List) is selected at the top of the menu. It should appear in blue, as shown here.

4 The Name box shows how your new favorite will be labeled in the Favorites list. Often the name of the site will be filled in for you by default. In some cases, the name might be very long or even quite different from what you expected. You can change this to something you'll recognize easily. The text in the Name box should appear highlighted in blue. If it is, you'll be able to start typing a new name right away. If it isn't, move your mouse cursor to the box, click at the right end of the current text, and use the BACKSPACE key to erase it.

5 Type your preferred name for the site label. This might be a short name for the site, such as *No Starch*, or something helpful to remind you what you saved it for, such as *Computer Books*.

6 Click the **Add** button.

7 You should see that the "add to favorites" button is now yellow. This tells you the page has been successfully saved as a favorite.

RETURNING TO A FAVORITE SITE

Once you've added a web page to your list of favorites, you can use this list to find the site again! To return to a site in your Favorites list, follow these steps:

1 Click the **hub button**, which looks like three lines, as shown here.

2 The hub menu will open. Make sure that Favorites is selected (the star at the top of the menu), as shown. It should be selected automatically, but if it isn't, just click the star button once. You should see a list of all the sites that you've added to Favorites.

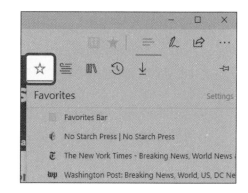

3 Click the site you would like to visit again (in this example, *The New York Times* site).

You should now see the page, as shown here.

DELETING A FAVORITE SITE

If you decide you no longer need a site in your Favorites list, you can easily remove it from the list using the following steps:

1 Click the **hub button**, highlighted next, to open the hub menu.

2 Right-click the favorite you want to remove.

3 Click the **Delete** button, highlighted here.

The site should now be gone from your Favorites list. You can still visit the site by typing the address; it just won't be listed in your Favorites list.

ACTIVITY #16

In this activity, you'll practice using Favorites to easily navigate to your favorite websites.

1. Add *www.nostarch.com* to your list of favorites.

2. Add *www.washingtonpost.com* to your list of favorites.

3. Use the favorites list to return to *www.nostarch.com*.

4. Remove *www.washingtonpost.com* from your list of favorites.

Sites to Explore

Now that you've learned how to look up a few different sites, you're ready to explore on your own. Start your journey with some of the following sites:

* **www.wikipedia.org:** An online encyclopedia with pages on thousands and thousands of topics. Whatever you're interested in finding out about, there is probably a Wikipedia page with information on it. Just type a term into the Wikipedia search box to get started.

* **www.yellowpages.com:** A directory for local businesses.

* **www.aarp.org:** This site contains useful news, videos, and resources for seniors.

* **www.skillfulsenior.com:** You can improve your mouse and keyboard skills here.

* **www.bestforpuzzles.com:** You can exercise your brain with crosswords, puzzles, and other games on this site.

Phew, We Did It!

In this lesson, we looked at browsing the internet. You navigated to web addresses, printed an interesting web page, and added sites to your Favorites list for easy access. In this lesson, you learned to do the following:

* Open Microsoft Edge

* Understand the parts of a web address

* Navigate to a site

* Move between pages by clicking links

* Go backward and forward to pages you've visited using the back and forward buttons

* Close tabs you don't want open

* Print web pages of interest

* Add sites to your Favorites list

In Lesson 6, you'll learn how to find websites, information, and pictures by searching the internet.

LESSON REVIEW

Congratulations! You've completed Lesson 5. Take this time to review what you've learned by completing the following tasks. If you can complete all of these tasks with confidence, then you're ready for Lesson 6. If not, don't lose heart; just keep practicing!

1. Open **Microsoft Edge**.

2. Navigate to the *Los Angeles Times* site (*www.latimes.com*).

3. Click an article to read it.

4. Print the article.

5. Return to the *Los Angeles Times* home page.

6. Add the *Los Angeles Times* to your Favorites list.

7. Close Microsoft Edge.

8. Open **Microsoft Edge** again and return to the *Los Angeles Times* page using the Favorites list.

LESSON 6
EXPLORING THE INTERNET

Now let's delve deeper and search the internet for
websites to meet your every need.

In Lesson 5, you learned that every website has a unique address known as a web address. But you won't always know the address of a particular website. For example, you may want to find new recipes for a delectable triple chocolate mud cake but not know the address of a website with that recipe.

In such a case, you'll need to use a search engine to search the internet. Searching is a very handy skill, as you'll see! In this lesson, you'll search for information on topics that interest you, such as recipes, car reviews, or puppy training advice. You'll then learn how to find images on the internet, and we'll look at a few popular sites you might want to explore.

Using a Search Engine

You can search the internet using a *search engine*, which is a website (with an address that's very easy to learn and remember!) that helps you locate other websites using a descriptive word or phrase. These descriptive words are known as *keywords*. You can use a search engine to find websites with gardening tips, nutritional information, stock prices, or anything you can think of.

You might have heard of a few different search engines, such as Google and Yahoo. This lesson focuses on how to use Microsoft's own search engine: Bing. We'll examine how to conduct a search, choose a website from the list of results, and refine a search!

CREATING A SEARCH

Good news! The address bar you learned to use in Lesson 5 is the same tool you'll use to search the internet. In this section, we'll search the internet for cake recipes as our first example. Simply follow these steps:

1. Open **Microsoft Edge** from the taskbar or the Start menu. Look back at "Opening Microsoft Edge" on page 116 if you're having trouble finding Microsoft Edge.

2. Type **cake recipes** into the address bar.

3 You might see a list of search suggestions appear as you type. These suggestions show you other common searches using those keywords to try to help you narrow down what you want. If any of the suggestions match what you're looking for, you can click them to search for those terms. For now, though, we'll stick with our "cake recipes" search.

4 Press ENTER.

You should now see a list of search results for cake recipes, as shown in the following figure.

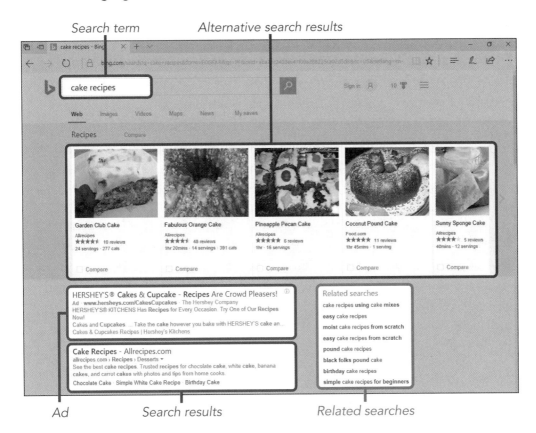

Search term   Alternative search results

Ad   Search results   Related searches

EXAMINING THE RESULTS PAGE

Let's break this screen down a little and look at the individual parts. Depending on the words you've searched for, your location, and other factors, your results might look a little different.

Alternative Search Results

Across the top of the screen in the gray section, you might see a strip of pictures showing recipes for similar cakes. These are suggestions from Bing based on similar things other people have searched for. Clicking an image would change your search results to match that image, but we won't do that now, since we want to stick to our "cake recipes" search.

This bar will not always appear, but when it does, the images and results will depend on what you've searched for. For example, if you were to search for "action movies," you'd see a list of popular action movies.

Ads and Related Search Terms

For many popular searches, you're likely to see a number of ads directly below the gray bar. These are websites that have paid a substantial amount of money to Bing to appear first when you search for certain words. This doesn't necessarily mean they're bad sites, but they may not be as relevant as the real search results further down the page and may be trying to sell you something. You can recognize ads because they have "Ad" written next to them in small gray text.

To the right of the search results, you'll see a list of related searches. These are search terms that Bing thinks might be good alternatives to what you've searched for, in case your results aren't quite what you wanted. There might also be more ads shown below the list of related searches, as well as at the bottom of the page.

The Search Results

The list in the center should be your search results. These are links to the web pages that Bing thinks are most relevant and useful to your search, and may include articles, pictures, videos, and recent news related to your search terms.

Ten results (plus ads, news, and the gray bar) are displayed on each Bing page, and you can scroll down the page to see all of the results. If you scroll all the way down to the bottom, you can click the **next button** to see the next page of results.

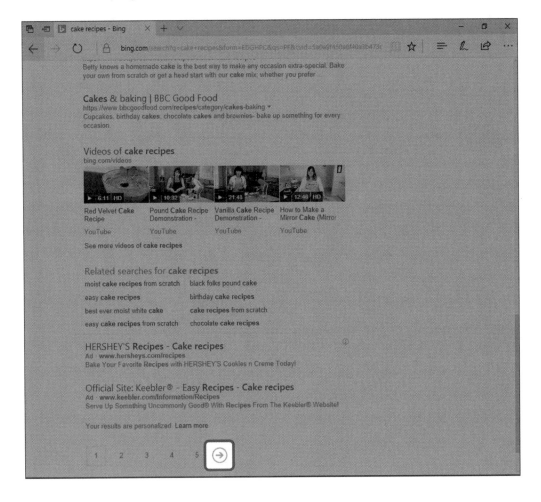

Not everyone will see the same results, even though they may have searched for identical information. Bing will use information such as the country you reside in and websites you've visited previously to try to decide which results suit you best, and it will list the results in that order. For example, if someone living in Australia searches for information about local veterinarians, they will see very different search results than someone living in Germany will.

OPENING A SEARCH RESULT

After you've created a search, it's time to examine your results and choose a link to the site you like the look of. Let's take a closer look at an individual search result, shown next.

The large blue heading is a link you can click to take you to the page that will hopefully contain the recipes you're searching for. Underneath the blue heading, in green, is the address of the linked website. This gives you a clue about the website where Bing found content related to your search. In this example, Bing has found cake recipes on a Martha Stewart website. Finally, beneath the green writing, there is a description of the page itself, which can help you decide whether it meets your needs.

To open a result, follow these steps:

1. Move down the search page until you find a result that sounds appealing.

2. Click the blue heading—this is the link that will open the website. In our example, we're going to open "24 Easy Cake Recipes | Martha Stewart" (if this didn't show up in your list, just pick a different result).

You should be taken to the site, which will look something like this:

You may see a different image if the site has been updated since we visited. Feel free to have a look around the page.

FINDING A DIFFERENT SEARCH RESULT

Skim through the information on the page you opened to decide if it's what you're looking for. If it doesn't quite meet your expectations, you can return to your search results and open a different result. Here's how:

1   Click the **back button** (highlighted next) to return to the list of search results.

2 When returning to your list of results, you might notice that the link you clicked previously is now purple. This tells you that the page has already been visited so you won't accidentally open the same link!

3 Read the description in a different search result. You may need to read several until you find one you like the look of.

4 Click the heading link of a search result to open another page. Read the page, and if it isn't quite what you were looking for, repeat these steps to keep searching for a result that works for you.

If none of the search results contains the information you're after, click back in the address bar and type a different search term.

ACTIVITY #17

In this activity, you're going to practice crafting your own Bing searches to find the answers to the following questions. Remember that it's best not to use full sentences.

* What is the biggest city in Australia?

* Who was president of the United States immediately before Abraham Lincoln?

* What should I feed my pet rabbit?

* What foods reduce cholesterol levels?

Searching for Images

You've seen how to use Bing to find information; now we'll look at finding images. Let's say you're interested in decorating a fantastic cake and are looking for some inspiration. Finding images of beautifully decorated cakes could give you some great ideas!

To search for images, follow these steps:

1 Open **Microsoft Edge**.

2 Type the search term **cake decorating** into the address bar, just like when you were searching for information.

3 Press ENTER. You should now see the search results for "cake decorating."

4 In the toolbar, click the **Images** button, highlighted here.

5 You should now see a page full of images that match your "cake decorating" search.

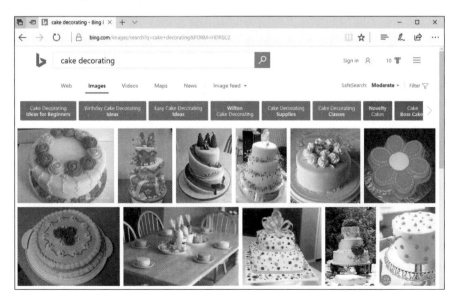

6 Click an image once to make it larger.

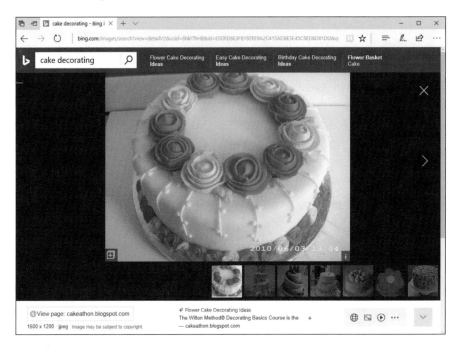

Remember, you can always return to the list of results by using the back button in the top-left corner of the screen. Try refining your image search to see what other images you can find.

ACTIVITY #18

In this activity, you'll find and print a picture you like.

1. Search Bing Images for anything you like (for example, a cake in the shape of a car).

2. Choose an image you like, and open it on its own in a new tab.

3. Print the image.

4. Close the tab showing the image.

5. Use the **View page** button to see what website the image came from.

Explore: Google

As mentioned earlier, Bing is just one of many different search engines. The most popular search engine available is Google, so if you can't find something using Bing or would just like to have an alternative, give Google a try! You can get to Google by typing **www.google.com** into your address bar. You could also search for "google" in your Bing search bar and click the link that matches that address.

A Google search works just like a Bing search—simply type the word or phrase you're looking for into the Google search box and press ENTER to see the results. Try performing a few Google searches to get the hang of it. You can also see that Google has an Images button, just like Bing does. How do the results compare with Bing's? How do you like the way the results are presented? If you find you prefer Google, feel free to use it from now on.

Explore: Facebook

Facebook is a popular social networking site designed to help you share information, photos, videos, news, and more with friends and family online. You can stay up-to-date with the grandkids, get in touch with long-lost school friends, or even discuss your favorite topics with strangers in various hobby groups. To get to Facebook, enter **www.facebook.com** into your address bar.

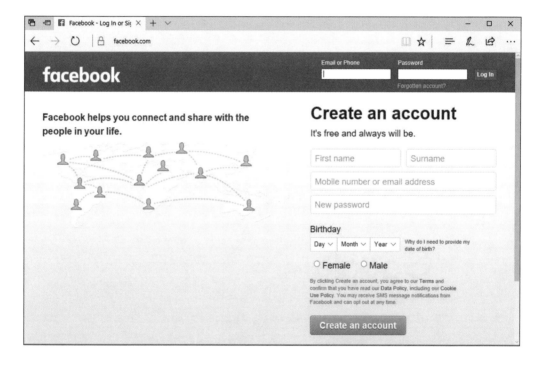

Facebook requires that you set up a free account to use it, so the first time you visit Facebook, you'll need to enter your information underneath the heading "Create an account." After you've done that, you'll be able to find friends and family members you want to keep in touch with. And whenever you return to Facebook, you can log in to your account using the login fields and button at the top-right corner of the page. For help setting up and navigating Facebook, take a look at *Facebook for Seniors*, available at *www.nostarch.com*.

Explore: Amazon

Amazon is the world's largest online store. You can buy a wide variety of products on Amazon, including books, electronics, jewelry, bits and bobs for the house, and much, much more. To start exploring Amazon, enter **www.amazon.com** into your address bar.

You can browse Amazon without an account, but in order to actually buy something, you'll need to sign up. Search for a particular item by entering search terms into the search box at the top of the page, or browse through the various categories by moving your mouse over the "Departments" heading.

Once you've found a product you like the look of, you can click it to show more information about it. If you decide you want to buy it, click the **Add to cart** button and then click **Proceed to checkout**. At this point, you should be asked to sign up for an account to proceed with your order, so enter the information you're being asked for. Be aware that for most products, you'll be charged a delivery fee, which will only be added to your total once you get to the checkout page. Once you've signed up, you can work your way through the checkout process by providing a delivery address and payment details.

Keep in mind that you can add multiple items to your cart before checking out so that you can order multiple things at once.

Online Shopping Tips

Some websites you're likely to explore, such as Amazon, involve making payments online. Usually you'll make online payments by creating an account for the site and entering your credit card details. While online payments are nothing to be frightened about, there are a few pointers you should always keep in mind to avoid becoming the victim of a scam:

* **Make sure you trust the site you're using.** Anyone can start up a site and take payments online, so it can be worth looking at reviews before entering any payment details. You can do this through a search engine by entering the site's main name and then the word *review*.

* **Look for the padlock in the address bar.** Shown here, the padlock should appear on any page for which you're typing in passwords or credit card information. This icon means that the site is secure, and details that you enter are much less likely to be stolen by a third party.

* **Make sure your computer is virus free.** Viruses can be used to steal payment details you type into your computer. For details about using antivirus apps that protect against viruses, flip to Lesson 14.

* **Use strong passwords to prevent anyone from getting into your accounts.** Strong passwords should be at least eight characters long and consist of a mix of lowercase and uppercase letters, numbers, and other characters. Examples of strong passwords might be *11Horses&Jockeys* or *Scarlett4Opera#*. Don't use information that someone else could guess, such as your pet's name or street name, and *definitely* don't use the word *password*!

* **Check your credit card statements regularly.** If you find a transaction you don't recognize, contact your bank immediately.

With these precautions in mind, let's take a quick look at some popular and interesting sites that can take payments and that you might like to explore on your own.

Phew, We Did It!

In this lesson, we looked at searching for a website and using Bing Images, and took a tour of the most popular sites on the internet. You learned the following:

* How to search for a website using Bing

* Strategies for finding helpful websites

* How to find images using Bing Images

* Some popular websites to explore on your own

In the next lesson, you'll learn how to watch videos on the internet.

LESSON REVIEW

Congratulations! You've completed Lesson 6. Take this opportunity to review what you've learned by completing the following tasks. If you can complete all of these tasks with confidence, you're ready for Lesson 7. If not, just keep practicing and find new sites to explore!

1. Use Bing to find some tips about how to housebreak a puppy. Explore the different results.

2. Use Bing to find some more online safety tips.

3. Use Bing Images to find some pictures that you could put in a birthday card.

4. Print an image or page that you like.

LESSON 7
WATCHING TV AND VIDEOS ONLINE

These days, you can watch TV shows, movies, and a variety of entertaining and useful videos using the internet!

In this lesson, you'll learn to watch videos on YouTube, a site with millions of videos available for free. Whether you want to hear Jane Fonda speak, learn how to change a tire, or watch a comedy show, you can do it all with your computer!

Watching Videos on YouTube

YouTube features millions of videos added by other people on the internet. On the YouTube website, you'll find everything from clips of old TV shows to instructional videos showing how to fix your car, decorate a cake, or even upload your own YouTube video!

PLAYING A VIDEO

To begin exploring YouTube, follow these steps:

1   Open **Microsoft Edge** from the taskbar or the Start menu.

2   Type the address **www.youtube.com** into the address bar and press ENTER. You can also search for "youtube" in the Microsoft Edge search bar, as you learned in Lesson 6, and then click the link that matches this address.

3   YouTube's website should appear as shown in the following figure. Your page may look different because YouTube's main page shows you a selection of videos it thinks you might like based on videos you've watched previously. If you haven't watched any videos yet, it will likely show you the most popular videos in your region. Over time, YouTube's suggestions should reflect your preferences.

4   To view a video, click one that looks interesting on the YouTube home page. We'll use the "Elton John Carpool Karaoke" video for this example, but you'll probably have different videos on your page.

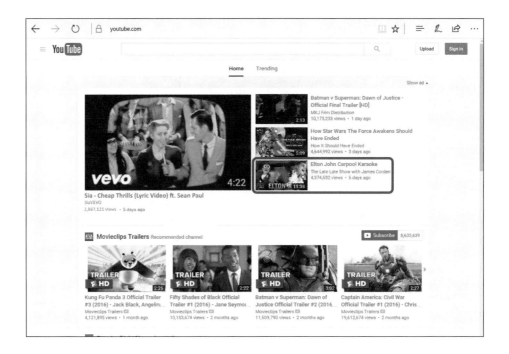

5 This link takes you to a page where your video loads and starts playing automatically. Keep in mind that a commercial might play before your actual video starts. YouTube makes money from advertisers who pay for their commercials to be shown before videos. After a few seconds into the commercial, you can sometimes skip it by clicking the Skip Ad button; if not, you may have to wait for the ad to finish playing.

MEETING THE VIDEO PAGE

The video should play automatically, but there are other functions of the video you'll want to learn! For example, you can use the pause button to pause the video, the volume control to make the video louder or quieter, and the expand button to make the video larger. The following figure highlights the important parts of the video page.

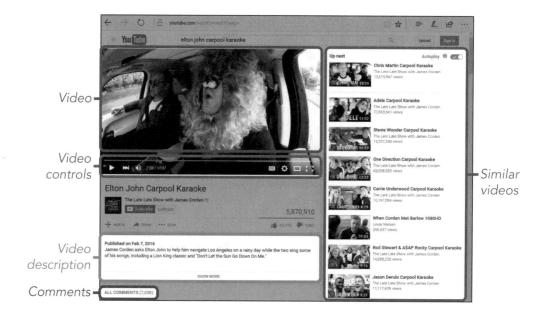

Video

Video controls

Similar videos

Video description

Comments

These are the different sections of the screen:

* **Video:** This is the part of the screen where your video should play automatically.

* **Video controls:** These buttons let you play, pause, and otherwise control the video. (More on these in the next section.)

* **Video description:** This is a summary of the video. You can click "Show More" to read more information, if there's more.

* **Similar videos:** This is a list of other videos you might like to see based on your choice of this video. You can click any one of these videos to go to that video's page, and it will start playing. The video at the top of this list, titled "Up next," should play automatically once the current video finishes.

* **Comments:** If you scroll down, you should see comments made about the video by other YouTube users.

YOUTUBE VIDEO CONTROLS

The video controls play, pause, and otherwise adjust your video. Let's take a look at them now.

Progress bar
    Volume control
    Next video *Timer*
Play/pause button
    Theater mode
    Subtitles
    Settings
    Full screen

* **Progress bar:** This bar shows the length of the video. The red section of the bar shows how much of the video you've watched.

* **Timer:** A timer underneath shows the length of the video (5 minutes, 8 seconds long) and how much of it you've already watched (18 seconds).

* **Play/pause button:** This button stops the video. Once pressed, it changes to a play button, which you can click to resume the video.

* **Next video:** This button skips the current video and starts the next one in the "Up next" list on the right side of your screen.

* **Volume control:** This control lets you turn the volume up or down. Hover your mouse cursor over this button to bring up a slider. You can click the white line and drag it to the right to turn up the volume or left to turn it down. Clicking the volume button mutes the video. Clicking the volume button again unmutes the video.

* **Subtitles:** This turns on subtitles/closed captions for the video, if they're available. Subtitles can be terrific if you're having difficulty hearing the video, but note that not all videos have subtitles available. If subtitles aren't available, this button won't appear.

* **Settings:** This option lets you control the video's quality settings. YouTube chooses the best settings automatically, so we won't look at this in detail.

* **Theater mode:** This button makes the video screen bigger.

* **Full screen:** This button gives you the cinematic experience! Click this button, and the video will take up your entire screen so that you can see it clearly. Once clicked, this button should change to the exit full screen button. Clicking it should return your video to normal size. You can also return to the normal-sized video by pressing the ESC key on your keyboard.

ACTIVITY #19

In this activity, you'll practice playing a YouTube video and adjusting some of its controls. Before you begin, return to the YouTube home page by clicking the **back button**.

1. Start watching a video.

2. Adjust the volume to a suitable level.

3. Pause the video.

4. Resume playing the video.

5. Put the video into full screen mode.

6. Return the video to normal size.

7. Watch another video from the list of similar videos.

8. Return to the YouTube home page.

SEARCHING FOR A YOUTUBE VIDEO

The list of videos on the YouTube home page is quite limited. Only a few dozen can fit on this screen, but YouTube has literally billions of videos to choose from! With the search feature, you can find a particular video or many videos on a particular topic. To search for a video, follow these steps:

1   Click in the search box at the top of any YouTube page.

2   Type a few words that describe the type of video you're looking for. In the following example, we use "cake decorating."

3   Click the **search button** or press the ENTER key.

4   This should bring up a list of results, as shown here.

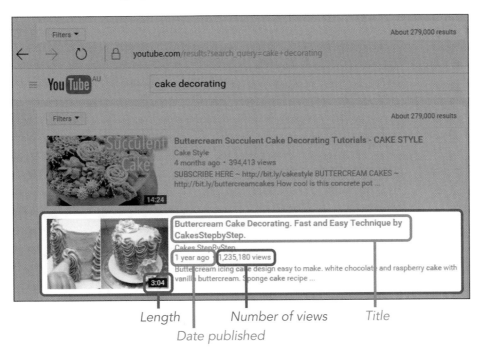

Length   *Number of views*   *Title*

Date published

5 Next to each video, you should see some useful information, including the length of the video, a brief description, the date it was published on YouTube, and its total number of views. This information can help you choose the video you want! For example, you might not want to sit through a two-hour documentary, or you might only be interested in videos created this year.

6 Click the video you want to watch.

When you've finished watching the video (or if it's not what you were looking for), you can either choose another video from the list of similar videos on the right side of the screen or click the back button to return to the search results.

ACTIVITY #20

In this activity, you'll practice searching for and opening a specific video on YouTube.

1. Search for videos on how to change a car tire.

2. Watch a video. Now you know how to change a tire!

Explore: TED Talks

The TED (technology, education, design) website features a variety of presentations by innovative leaders in the fields of business, academia, entertainment, politics, and more. The topics vary, but all are designed to be informative, entertaining, and thought-provoking. Best of all, these presentations, called TED Talks, are completely free and available to watch anytime!

To watch a TED Talk, enter **www.ted.com** into your address bar, press
ENTER, and then click any video that looks interesting to play it.

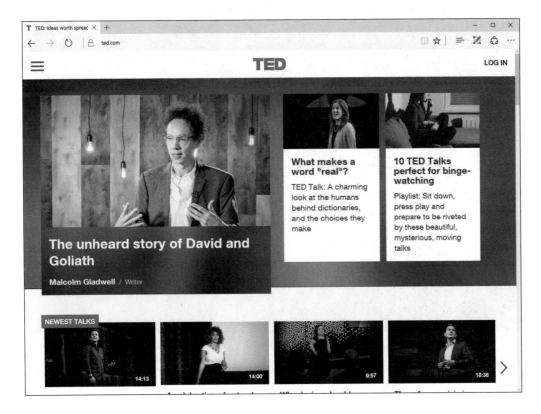

Explore: Netflix

Netflix is a popular website that lets you watch a huge range of movies
and TV shows online, whenever you like. This is known as *streaming*.
It's so popular that more than 50 million American households have
subscribed to Netflix.

Unfortunately, unlike YouTube and TED Talks, it's not completely free;
Netflix requires a monthly subscription fee, but you can watch as many
movies and shows as you like as a subscriber. You can try it for free for a
month, and if you don't want to keep it after the trial period is over, you
can cancel your subscription at no cost.

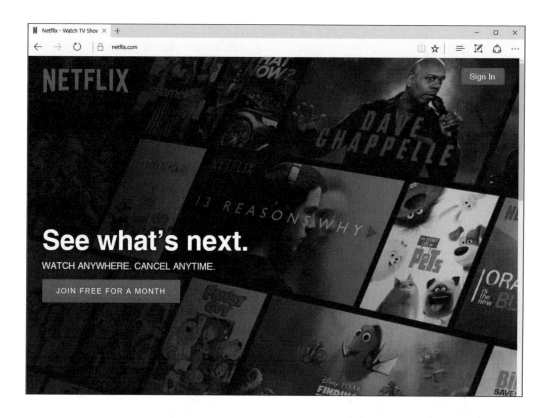

You need to provide payment details to use Netflix, even for the free trial, so it's worth flipping back to "Online Shopping Tips" on page 150.

To sign up for Netflix, follow these steps:

1   From Microsoft Edge, type **www.netflix.com** in the address bar, or search for "netflix" and find the correct link.

2   Click **JOIN FREE FOR A MONTH** and then type the information requested, including your payment information.

After you create an account and sign in, you should be able to see the entire range of movies and TV shows available on Netflix. You can scroll down to see the different categories. Use the left and right arrows to see more results within each category. You can also use the search box at the top of the page to look for a particular title or actor.

Explore: Crackle

Crackle is another online streaming site, run by Sony. Like Netflix, it contains a range of movies and TV shows you can watch from your computer. There aren't as many titles available, but Crackle is completely free to use and is funded by advertisements rather than a subscription fee. You can watch videos without even having to sign up, or you can create an account and let Crackle recommend videos it thinks you'll like.

Phew, We Did It!

In this lesson, we looked at some exciting websites you can use to watch videos. In particular, you learned how to do the following:

* Watch a YouTube video

* Search YouTube to find specific videos

In the next lesson, you'll learn how to download apps to make your computer do even more.

LESSON REVIEW

Congratulations! You've completed Lesson 7. Take this opportunity to review what you've learned by completing the following tasks. If you can complete all of these tasks with confidence, you're ready for Lesson 8. If not, just keep practicing!

1. Play a popular video from the main YouTube page.

2. Use YouTube to find and play a trailer for your favorite film or an upcoming film you've heard about.

LESSON 8

DOWNLOADING NEW APPS

Discover how to add new apps to your computer to get it to do more!

Back in Lesson 2, we looked at using some of the most popular apps that come included on your computer, such as the Microsoft Solitaire Collection, the Calendar app, and the Weather app. In this lesson, you'll continue your journey through the world of apps by learning to find and add new apps so that you can explore apps on your own and download the ones that suit you!

Why Add More Apps?

The apps on your computer can be fun and useful, but they are not always specific to you and your needs. An important part of making your computer more useful and enjoyable is ensuring that you've found the tools you'll use most for work and fun. The Store has a wonderful variety of apps that will suit you and your lifestyle. In the Store, you can find apps to help you with the following activities:

* Reading books on your computer

* Finding recipes

* Tracking your nutritional intake

* Organizing invoices

* Creating presentations and budgets

* Storing passwords

* Learning a language

* Creating greeting cards and artwork

* Keeping a diary

* Selling your house

* Playing games

The Store

Apps can be found and added to your computer from the Store. This isn't a real brick-and-mortar store but rather an app that comes installed on your computer and helps you find other apps.

Although there are many free apps in the Store, not everything you'll find there is free. In addition to paid apps, the Store also showcases movies, music, and TV shows that you can purchase or rent. In this lesson, we'll only look at apps, and we'll focus on apps that are free!

MEETING THE STORE

The Store is home to thousands of new apps just waiting to be discovered! To access the Store, follow these steps:

1 Click the **start button** in the bottom-left corner of the screen.

2 Click **Store**, highlighted next (if you can't see the Store app tile, type **store** to find it).

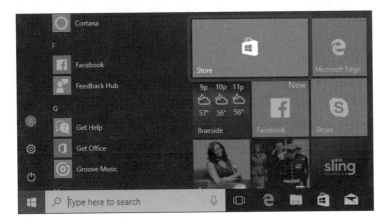

3 You should now see the main Store screen, shown next. The apps and products offered will change frequently, so your screen might look a little different.

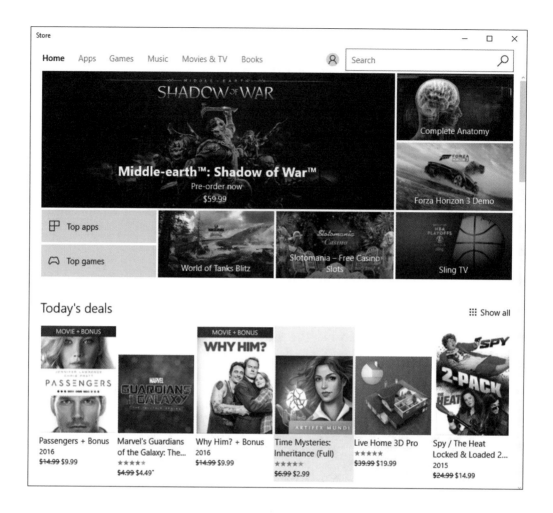

You'll notice a list of sections along the top of the screen: Home, Apps, Games, Music, Movies & TV, and Books. You can think of these like departments in a store. Here, they break down the Store as follows:

* **Home:** This section is where you'll start when you first open the Store; it contains a selection of the most popular apps, games, music tracks, movies, TV shows, and books from the other sections. The choices shown here are updated regularly, so you'll likely see a different selection each time you open the Store.

* **Apps:** This section holds the different apps you can install on your computer, with the exception of games, which have their own section.

* **Games:** Because so many games are available to download, they have their own section separate from apps. You can install games from here.

* **Music:** This section lets you purchase music tracks and albums.

* **Movies & TV:** Here you can find a large selection of the latest movies and TV shows for purchase. The Store will even allow you to rent many movies and give you a limited time in which you can watch them.

* **Books:** This section lets you purchase ebooks.

We'll just look at the Apps and Games departments as we continue exploring the Store.

FINDING APPS AND GAMES

The Store has many thousands of apps, which can make finding the perfect app a little tricky! To make things easier, there are two main ways of finding apps, as shown next:

* **Categories:** If you're not sure of the name of the app you're looking for, or if you just want to browse and see what's available, you can use the categories to find apps of a particular type.

* **Search:** If you know the name of a specific app you want to download (for example, Netflix), you can use the Search feature to easily find that exact app.

Because the Store has so many great games, it has a separate Games department, but you can search for games in the exact same way you search for apps: by category or by searching for a specific game.

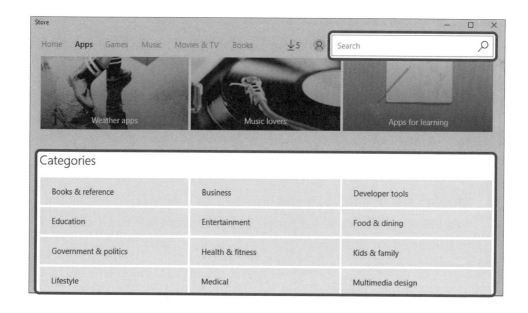

SEARCHING USING CATEGORIES

Searching for apps or games by category is a great way to have a look at what's available and find an app or game you'll like. In this example, we will search for an app by category (you can use the same method to search for games, too). Follow these steps:

1 From the buttons at the top of the Store, click **Apps**. (If you're searching for a game by categories, click **Games** instead.)

2 This will open the Apps section of the Store, which will present many popular and featured apps, as shown next.

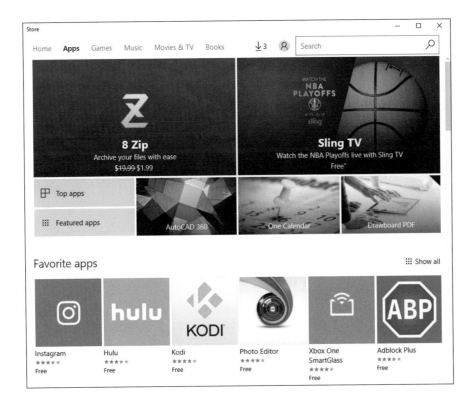

3   Scroll to the bottom of the page using the scroll bar to find a list of app categories. These categories represent the different types of apps available in the Store.

4   Click the app category that interests you. For this example, click the **Food & dining** category.

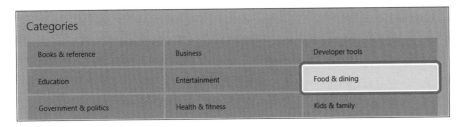

5   The "Food & dining" category apps will now appear. You might see a different list of apps than in the example shown next.

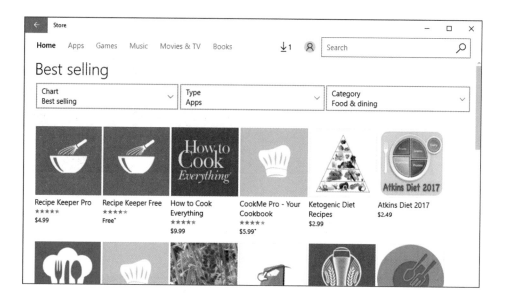

6   Notice the star rating underneath each app. This gives you a quick idea of how other people have reviewed the app. Apps with four or five stars have been rated highly by other people who used them; conversely, you might want to avoid apps with only one or two stars.

7   The Store will start by showing you the most popular free apps, but further refining your search to show apps that are highly rated or new can be very helpful. You can refine your choices by clicking the **Chart** option in the top-left corner of the screen, which gives a list of choices.

8   To browse only free apps, click the **Chart** box and then click **Top free** from the list that appears. Many excellent and high-quality apps are free, so don't hesitate to explore this option. But be wary, because even though the apps are free, they may contain *in-app purchases*, which means you will be prompted to buy things with real money when you use them (for example, to add features or remove advertising). If an app lists **Free⁺** rather than just **Free** beneath its rating, that means it has in-app purchases. We'll look at this topic a bit more later in the lesson.

ACTIVITY #21

In this activity, we're going to practice browsing the categories and refining a search.

1. In the Store, browse the Education category of apps.

2. Refine your list to only free apps.

SEARCHING USING THE SEARCH BOX

If you know the name of the app you want, searching for that name is the quickest way to go. For example, if you wanted to find the TuneIn Radio app, which you might have seen advertised on television, you'd search for "TuneIn Radio" in the Search box, and a list of apps with similar names would appear. Then you'd just choose the one with the correct name.

You can also search for keywords using this box; for example, if you wanted a radio app but didn't know the name of a particular one, you could just search for "radio" in the box, and it would bring up a list of apps with the word *radio* in either the name or description.

We'll search for a popular recipe app, So Cookbook. Follow these steps:

1 Click in the **Search** box in the top-right corner of the screen.

2 Type the name of the app or game you want to search for into the Search box (in this case, **So Cookbook**) and then press ENTER or click the magnifying glass icon.

3 A list of apps and games matching your search will appear. Your results may be slightly different from the following figure, as more apps and games are added to the Store all the time. You can also use the **Type** box at the top of the screen to narrow down the results to just apps or games.

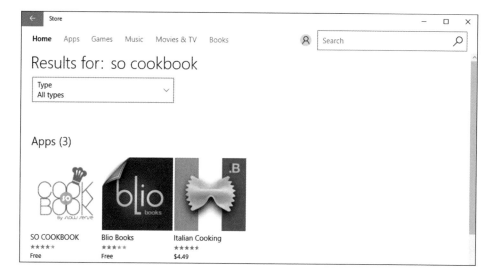

Choosing an App or Game

As our searches have shown, the Store has lots of great apps and games! So how do you know which ones are right for you? You need more information about an app before you choose whether to install it.

Once you've done your search for "So Cookbook," click the tile of the app from the search results, shown here. Information about the app will then appear, as shown in the figure on the next page.

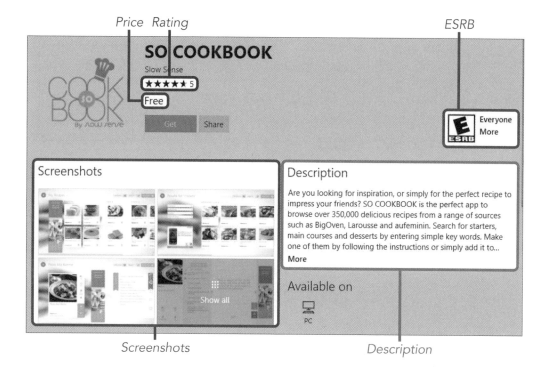

Price   Rating

SO COOKBOOK

Slow Sense

★★★★★ 5

Free

Get   Share

ESRB

E Everyone
More
ESRB

Screenshots

Show all

Description

Are you looking for inspiration, or simply for the perfect recipe to impress your friends? SO COOKBOOK is the perfect app to browse over 350,000 delicious recipes from a range of sources such as BigOven, Larousse and aufeminin. Search for starters, main courses and desserts by entering simple key words. Make one of them by following the instructions or simply add it to...

More

Available on

PC

Screenshots   Description

* **Price:** This appears toward the top of the screen and will either say *Free* or list a price, such as $3.99.

* **Rating:** It's helpful to know how popular the app is with other customers. The rating goes from one to five stars. The number beside the stars tells you how many users have given a rating and review. If the app has lots of reviewers, the rating is probably more reliable than if the app has only one or two reviewers.

* **ESRB:** The Entertainment Software Rating Board (ESRB) assigns age ratings to apps based on their content.

* **Screenshots:** These show you some pictures from the app itself so that you can see what it will look like.

* **Description:** This tells you what the app can do and what it's useful for. Sometimes the last part of the description is hidden; to see the full description, you can click **More**.

If you like the look of the app, then you're ready to install and enjoy it! However, if the app doesn't quite seem right to you, you can use the Search box to find a different app, or you can click the back button to return to other apps in the category.

Installing an App

Once you've found an app you like and have read its description page, you can install it. We'll use the So Cookbook app as an example. Here's how to install an app:

1 Click the **Get** button, as highlighted below.

2 The app will begin to download and install, and the Get button will change into a *progress bar*, which is a visual indicator of how much of the app has been installed and how much is left to install, thus giving you an idea of how long it will take. Depending on the speed of your internet connection, it might take a couple of minutes to download and install the app. Once the progress bar is finished, you'll be told that the app has been successfully installed, as shown in the next figure.

3 Click the **Launch** button to open the app.

ACTIVITY #22

In this activity, you'll find and install a fun game called Microsoft Jigsaw.

1. Find the **Microsoft Jigsaw** game in the Store.

2. Install the game.

3. Start the app.

Reopening an App

When you install an app for the first time, a convenient Launch or Play button will appear in the Store, but that button doesn't stay there forever. Fortunately, you can open downloaded apps from the Start menu, just as you open apps like Store and Weather. Here are the steps to follow:

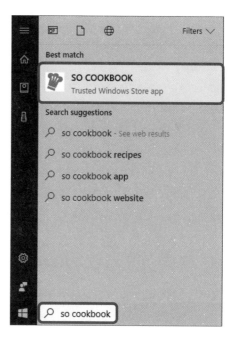

1. Click the **start button** or click in the **start search box**.

2. Type the name of the app you want to open (in this case, **so cookbook**).

3. Click the app to open it.

Your app will appear! If you don't remember the exact name of your app, you can click the **start button** and then scroll down the full list of apps on the left side of the Start menu and try to spot it, as shown next.

Removing an App

Sadly, even the greatest love affairs come to an end, and you might find it's time to delete an app. It's useful to delete things you don't use anymore to free up space on your computer for more things you do use—and to declutter your apps list in the Start menu to make it easier to find the apps you use. The amount of space you have on your computer to store things is limited, though usually you have enough for many apps and files. Having too many apps, however, can cause your computer to become slow and, in the worst case, limit your ability to add new files or install new apps.

Let's remove the So Cookbook app.

1. Click the **start button**.

2. Scroll down the list of apps until you find So Cookbook, or search for it in the search box—but don't click it yet!

3. Right-click **So Cookbook** to bring up a small menu.

4. Click the **Uninstall** button, shown in the following figure.

5   A box will pop up telling you that the app will be uninstalled.

6   Click **Uninstall** again to confirm.

The So Cookbook app will now be removed. You'll no longer find it in the Start menu, and all traces of it will be gone. If you decide you want the app back at any time, it's always possible to go back to the Store and install it again in just the same way you installed it the first time. Nonetheless, you should only uninstall apps if you've stopped using them altogether.

Explore: Paid Apps

So far, we've focused on apps that are free of charge, but the Store also contains many apps that you can purchase for a small fee. If you find an app that you must pay for before installing, you'll see a Buy button in place of the Get button. Above that, the price of the app should be stated clearly. Some apps also have a "Free trial" button, which will allow you to use the app for free for a short period of time before purchasing it.

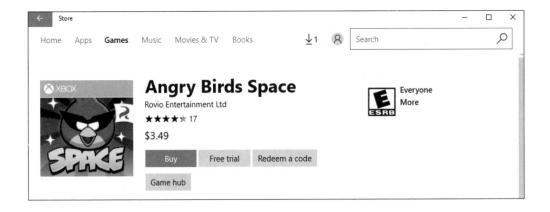

Once you click the Buy button, you'll be asked to enter your password. This is a security measure, to make sure it's really you trying to buy the app. The password will be the same password you use to log in to your computer when you first turn it on.

If this is the first time you've purchased an app, you'll then be asked to enter payment details, as shown here.

Many people make payments of these types by entering their credit card or debit card details, but there are other ways of making a payment in the Store. If you're not comfortable entering credit card details on your computer, you can purchase a Windows Store or Xbox Live gift card from a retailer such as Walmart. You can then simply click the **Redeem a gift card** button and type the code that's printed on the card. If you have a PayPal account, you can also use it to make purchases from the Store. Look back at "Online Shopping Tips" on page 150 for more information about safely making online payments.

Apps to Try

Now that you've learned how to download and install apps from the Store, here are a few to try out on your own:

* **Adblock Plus:** Prevents most ads from being displayed when you're browsing the internet. Unlike most apps, Adblock Plus integrates with Microsoft Edge, so you don't open it separately. When you open Edge after installing Adblock Plus, you should see a red ABP symbol in the top-right corner letting you know that ads are being blocked.

* **Candy Crush Saga:** A very popular (and addicting!) game.

* **LastPass:** Keeps track of all your passwords.

* **Translator:** Translates from one language to another—fantastic if you're going on vacation!

* **WatchESPN:** If you have a cable TV subscription, this app lets you watch ESPN from your computer.

Phew, We Did It!

In this lesson, we looked at how to search for, download, and uninstall apps and games from the Store. You learned how to do the following:

* Access the Store

* Find and install apps

* Remove unwanted apps from your computer

In the next lesson, you'll learn how to listen to music online for free.

LESSON REVIEW

Congratulations! You've completed Lesson 8. Take this opportunity to review what you've learned by completing the following tasks. If you can complete all of these tasks with confidence, you are ready for Lesson 9. If not, don't lose heart—just keep practicing!

1. Open the Store.

2. Install the Microsoft Mahjong game from the "Puzzle & trivia" category.

3. Play a game of Mahjong.

4. Uninstall Microsoft Mahjong.

LESSON 9

LISTENING TO MUSIC ONLINE

It's easy to listen to music and
even enjoy the radio using your computer!

In this lesson, you'll learn how to use the Spotify website to listen to millions of songs, both new and old, online.

Signing Up for Spotify

Spotify is a popular website for listening to music. It offers a free service that lets you listen to particular songs or artists, with the compromise that you have to listen to occasional advertisements between tracks. You can choose to pay a small monthly fee to subscribe to Spotify and get rid of these occasional ads.

Unlike most of the apps we've used in this book, Spotify requires you to create an account in order to use its service. The good news is that it's completely free to sign up. Navigate to Spotify's website to sign up for Spotify:

1 Open **Microsoft Edge** from the taskbar or the Start menu.

2 Type **play.spotify.com** into the address bar and press ENTER. This should bring up the Spotify Play page, shown here.

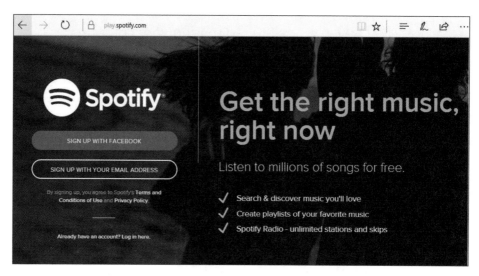

3 Click the **Sign up with your email address** button.

4 This should bring up the following sign-up form. Spotify will need some information from you in order to set up an individual account. This is useful because it lets Spotify keep track of the songs you've been listening to so that it can suggest other songs you might like.

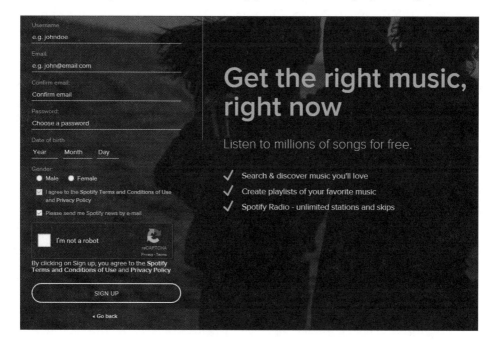

5 Click the **Username** box and enter the username you want to use on Spotify. This should be unique, so simple usernames such as "chris" and "carrie" are likely to be already taken. At the same time, your username should be simple enough to memorize because you'll need to type it in every time you use Spotify. You might try using some combination of your initials and surname; if that doesn't work, try adding a memorable number, too.

6 Click the **Email** box and enter your email address.

7 Click the **Confirm email** box and enter your email address again to make sure you typed it correctly the first time. If the two email addresses you entered don't match, you'll be notified to double-check your entries and correct any mistakes.

8 Click the **Password** box and enter a password that's easy for you to remember (because you'll need to enter it when you want to sign in to Spotify) but difficult for someone else to guess so that no one else can access your account. Ideally, your password should be a combination of letters and numbers that's at least eight characters long. When you type it into the Password box, your password will appear as dots to prevent someone nearby from seeing it.

9 Click the box labeled **Year** and choose your year of birth from the list, and then do the same for the month and day of your birth.

10 Click the circle next to Male or Female to select your gender.

11 By default, Spotify will send you occasional notifications by email. If you don't want to receive these notifications, uncheck the **Please send me Spotify news by e-mail** box.

12 Spotify needs to make sure you are a person and not a computer program that's automatically signing up for hundreds of accounts, so be sure to check the **I'm not a robot** box. You may be asked to perform a simple task, such as clicking the picture that has a cat in it, to prove you're not an automated program creating a fake account.

13 Click **Sign Up**. You may now be asked to accept the terms and conditions for Spotify. Click the **Terms and Conditions of Use** and **Privacy Policy** links to read them in detail if you like, and then click the **Agree** button, highlighted next, to continue.

14 Finally, you might be asked to enable Flash in order to access Spotify. Flash is a small program you sometimes need in order to access some video and audio content online. Click the **Click here to enable Flash** link, shown next, to do so. If you're then asked to allow Flash to always run on Spotify, click **Always Allow**.

> Please enable Flash to use the Spotify web player. **Click here to enable Flash**

This should take you back to the main Spotify Play page. Now that you have an account, let's see how to find music!

Using Spotify

Spotify provides two main ways of finding music. If you know what you're looking for, use the search feature to find a particular song, album, or artist. Alternatively, you can browse a list of selections and play songs from particular categories, such as classical music or pop songs.

SEARCHING FOR MUSIC

To find a particular song or artist, follow these steps:

1 Click the **Search** button on the left side of the page.

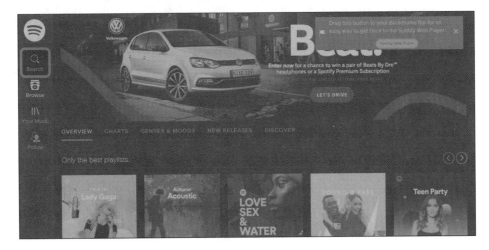

2 This will bring up a search box on the left side of the page, as shown here. Enter the name of a song or artist you want to find.

3 As you begin typing, a list of suggestions will appear below the search box. Click the desired result, as shown here.

4 This will open a list of relevant results for your search term on the right side of the screen. Many search results will be too long to display on a single screen, in which case you can scroll down to see more results. When you move your mouse over a song, you should see a small play button appear to the left of the song name, as shown next. Click the **play button** to begin playing the song.

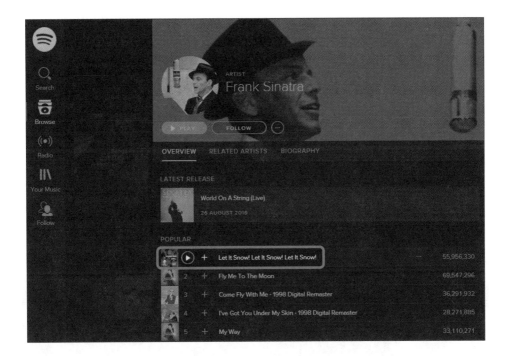

5 The song will now begin playing, and a panel will appear on the right with some controls you can use to pause and play the song. The arrow to the right of the pause button is the *skip* button. This lets you skip forward to the next song in the list, if you don't like the song you're currently listening to. To the left of the pause button is a *previous* button that lets you return to the previous song. This can be useful if you've accidentally skipped a song you like or if you just want to listen to a song a second time.

When the song finishes playing, Spotify automatically begins playing the next song in the list shown in the middle of the screen. To keep the list playing while you do other things, you can minimize Spotify. Look back at "Restoring Disappearing Apps" on page 45 for details about minimizing.

BROWSING FOR MUSIC

To browse different categories of music, follow these steps:

1 Click the **Browse** button on the left side of the page.

2 You will see headings for Charts, Genres & Moods, New Releases, and Discover in the middle of the page. These work as follows:

*   **Charts:** Lets you listen to the songs that are currently the most popular, either globally or in your particular country.

*   **Genres & Moods:** Lets you pick a particular genre of music, such as Classical, Country, or Jazz.

*   **New Releases:** Lets you listen to recently released albums and singles.

*   **Discover:** Lets you listen to music that Spotify thinks you'll enjoy, based on the songs you've already listened to. This is good to explore after you've played a few songs to let Spotify get to know what kind of music you like.

3 Click one of the headings. For this example, we'll choose **Genres & Moods**.

4 This brings up a list of music genres. You can scroll down to see more genres. Click your desired genre, such as **Classical**.

5 This brings up a selection of *playlists* in that genre. These playlists are collections of songs chosen by Spotify or other Spotify users. Click a playlist to see what songs it contains, as shown next.

6 You should see a brief description of the playlist as well as a list of the songs in the playlist. Click the green **Play** button at the top of the screen to play the entire playlist, or move your mouse over an individual song and click the **play button** next to it to play that song first.

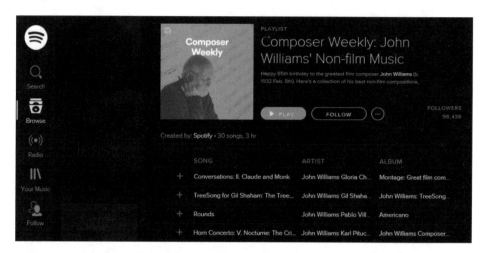

Once the song starts playing, you should see the set of controls appear on the right side of the page, allowing you to pause, skip, or replay songs. Remember that Spotify will automatically continue to the next song once the current song is finished.

ACTIVITY #23

In this activity, you'll practice navigating Spotify and play a song on the site.

1. Use the search feature to find songs by Billy Joel (or another artist, if you have one in mind) and play one of the songs in the search results.

2. Use the browse feature to find and play a jazz playlist.

Logging Back In to Spotify

Once you've exited the Spotify site, you may need to log back in the next time you want to use it again. Follow these steps to log in to Spotify again.

1   Open **Microsoft Edge**.

2   Type **play.spotify.com** into the address bar and press ENTER.

3   Click the **Already have an account? Log in here** button at the bottom left of the page. It's quite small, but it's there!

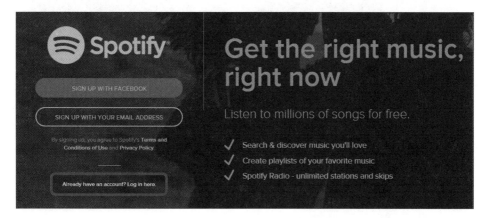

4   Click the **Username** box and enter the Spotify username you created earlier.

5   Click the **Password** box and enter the Spotify password you created earlier.

6   Check the **I'm not a robot** button. You may be asked to answer a simple question to prove that you're not a robot, as described earlier.

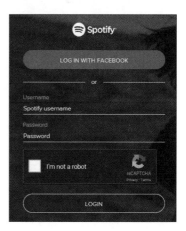

7   Click the **Login** button.

This should take you back to the main Spotify Play page, where you can use the Search or Browse button to find or discover the music you want.

Explore: Buying Songs

So far we've looked at listening to music online for free. However, if you want to keep a particular song or album on your computer, you can buy a digital version of it from the Store. The Store provides a way of buying songs and entire albums.

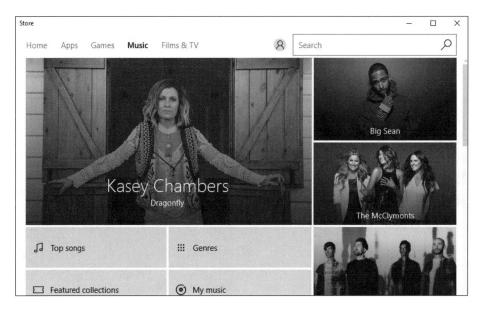

The process is identical to that of buying apps, so if you worked your way through Lesson 8, you should be well equipped to buy songs! You'll need to open the Store and click the Music tab at the top of the screen. You can then scroll through the music genres or search for songs or artists using the search bar in the top-right corner. You can also browse in the same way you browsed the Store for apps.

When you find a song or album you want to buy, click the price tag next to it to buy it. If you haven't already added payment details, you'll be asked to do so now—go to "Explore: Paid Apps" on page 179 for more information about entering payment information in the Store.

Once you've purchased a song, you can listen to it at any time using the Groove Music app, which you can get to using the Start menu. Just click the **My Music** heading to see all of your purchased songs and albums.

Explore: TuneIn Radio

TuneIn Radio lets you listen to all of your favorite radio stations, both locally and from around the world. You can use TuneIn Radio to listen to:

* Music

* Sports coverage

* Talk radio

* Prerecorded interviews and shows, known as *podcasts*

* Foreign radio stations

* Shows in other languages

* Audiobooks

The TuneIn Radio app is available for free from the Store, so simply download it and then start listening!

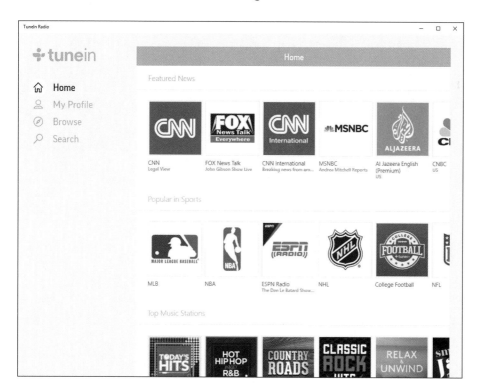

Phew, We Did It!

In this lesson, we explored listening to music online with the Spotify website. In this lesson, you learned how to do the following:

* Search for your favorite songs or artists on Spotify

* Browse different music genres on Spotify

* Log back in to Spotify

In the next lesson, you'll learn how to read books for free on your computer.

LESSON REVIEW

Congratulations! You've completed Lesson 9. Take this opportunity to review this lesson by completing the following tasks. If you can complete these tasks with confidence, you're ready for Lesson 10. If not, don't worry: just keep practicing!

1. Find music by your favorite artist on Spotify.

2. Listen to songs from your favorite music genre on Spotify.

LESSON 10
READING EBOOKS WITH OVERDRIVE

Now that you've learned how to listen to music online, let's explore another pastime you can enjoy using your computer: books!

OverDrive is an app that lets you borrow ebooks for free from your local library and read them from the comfort of your computer. It works just like borrowing a regular library book: the book is loaned for a certain amount of time, and if a book is already checked out, you have to wait for it to be returned. One big advantage is that OverDrive automatically returns the book for you, so there's no chance of paying any late fees! To use the OverDrive app, you need to be a member of a library that has signed up for OverDrive. With more than 30,000 libraries that use OverDrive in more than 40 countries, there's a good chance you'll find one near you.

Installing and Signing Up for OverDrive

You can download OverDrive from the Store. To do so, follow these steps:

1   Open the **Store** app from the Start menu. You should now see the main Store screen.

2   Type **OverDrive** into the Search box in the top-right corner of the Store and press ENTER.

3   Your OverDrive search results should appear. Click the **OverDrive - Library eBooks & Audiobooks** tile in the Apps section, highlighted next.

4   Click the **Get** button, highlighted next.

5 The app should start to download and install. Once it is finished, open OverDrive by clicking the **Launch** button, highlighted next.

✱ **NOTE:** *You can open OverDrive again in the future by entering* ***OverDrive*** *into the Start search box.*

6 This should bring up a sign-up screen. If this is the first time you're using OverDrive, you need to sign up for a free account. Click the **Sign Up** button, highlighted next.

7 Scroll down to the "Enter your details" section.

8 Click the **Name** box and enter your full name.

9 Click the **Email address** box and enter your email address. You need to enter your email address again in the next box to make sure you didn't mistype your email address.

10 Click the **Password** box, choose a password to use for OverDrive, and then enter it here. Your password needs to be at least eight characters long. Make sure it's something you can remember the next time you want to use OverDrive.

11 Your completed form should look something like the one shown here. Click the blue **Sign up** button to create your OverDrive account.

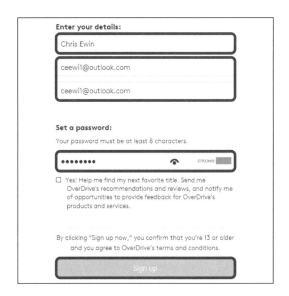

12 OverDrive will send you an email requesting that you verify your account, to make sure you provided your correct email address. Once you receive this email, click the verification link included to confirm your account. This will take you to the OverDrive website, where you'll have to click the **Verify** button. If you're having trouble with email, review Lesson 4.

Adding a Library to Borrow From

Now that you've created your OverDrive account, you need to add your library to your account. You can add more than one library, but you need to be a member of that library in order to borrow ebooks. After you add a library, it should always show up when you open OverDrive.

To add a library, follow these steps:

1 Click the **Add a library** button, highlighted here.

2 This should bring up the "Add a library" box on the right side of the screen. Enter the name of the library that you are a member of and click **Search**, highlighted next. If you'd prefer to see which libraries near you are available with OverDrive, click **Browse for libraries** instead. This will bring up a list of countries. From there, find yours and click it, which will bring up a list of states; click yours.

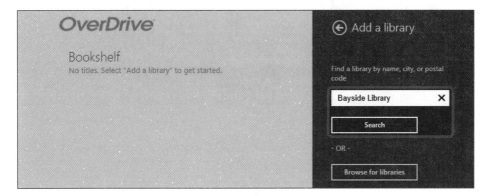

3 You should now see a list of libraries that match your search criteria. Arranged alphabetically, this list is probably quite long. Click your library when you find it.

4 Click the library again to add it to your list, highlighted next. For this example, I'll choose Bayside Library Service in Australia.

5 This should bring up your library's main page, which will look something like this:

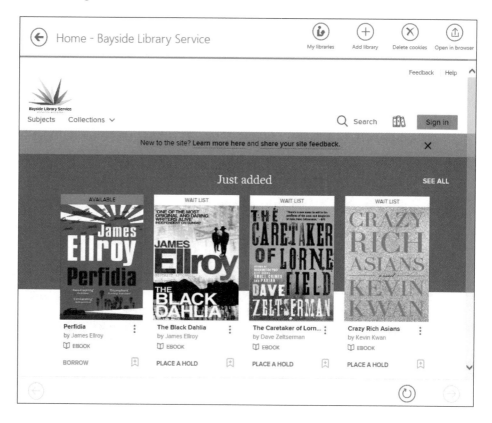

Now that you've added your library, it should always appear in your list of libraries whenever you open OverDrive. You can easily click the library from this list to open it.

Signing In to a Library

Before you can borrow a book, you need to sign in to your library using your library card number and PIN. Your library card number should be somewhere on your library card, and the PIN will be a number you chose with the library. If you don't know these details or aren't sure if you have them, check with your library directly.

To sign in to your library, follow these steps:

1 Click the **Sign in** button, as shown here.

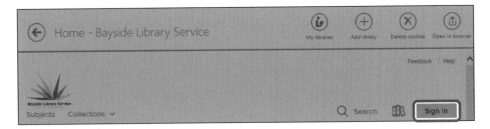

2 This will bring up the sign-in page, shown here. Type your card number and PIN into the appropriate boxes on the left side of the screen. You might also want to check the **Remember my card number on this device** box. That way, you don't need to re-enter your card number every time you borrow a book.

You'll then be taken back to your library's main page.

Finding and Borrowing a Book

OverDrive provides many different ways of finding books to borrow, and we'll focus on two easy methods here: searching and browsing. Once you've found a book you like, you can borrow and download it, which lets you read the book as often as you want for the period of the loan.

SEARCHING FOR A BOOK

If you know the name of the author or the title of the book you want to borrow, you can use the search feature to find it. Follow these steps:

1 Click the **Search** button, highlighted here. This will bring up the search box.

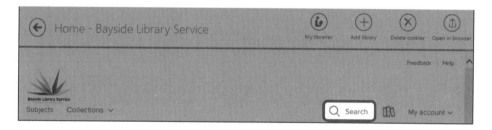

2 Type the name of the book or author you're looking for into the search box. As you type, OverDrive will suggest some options in a list below the search box. For example, in the following figure, Michael Connelly appears in the list of suggestions. You can select one of these options or simply press ENTER.

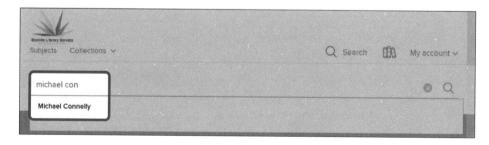

Entering a search term should bring up a list of search results, which we discuss next.

THE LIST OF RESULTS

Your listed results should look something like the following figure.

Cover   Availability

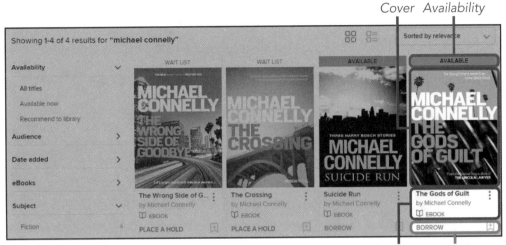

Title, author, and type   Borrow button

The results contain a lot of useful information:

❋ **Cover:** The front cover of the book is visible for each title. Clicking the cover takes you to a page that provides more information about the book.

❋ **Availability:** Books currently available should have the word "Available" written above their covers, and books currently on loan should say "Wait List."

❋ **Title:** The book's title is printed below the cover.

❋ **Author:** This shows you who wrote the book. Clicking the author's name will show you other books by the same author.

❋ **Type:** Most items should be ebooks, which contain written text that you can read on your computer. Your library may also offer a number of *audiobooks*, which are audio recordings of a book that you can listen to. These can be borrowed and downloaded exactly like ebooks.

* **Borrow button:** This button lets you borrow the book directly from the search results screen, without first reading more information about the book. If the book is currently on loan, this button will say "Place a Hold" instead. Clicking the **Place a Hold** button will let you reserve the book so that you're next in line when it's returned. If you place a hold on a book, you'll receive an email letting you know when the book is available.

Click the image for any book to get more information about it.

BROWSING FOR A BOOK

Sometimes you won't have a particular book in mind but want to see what's available. In that case, you may want to browse the titles your library offers in a particular genre. OverDrive has a browsing feature that lets you do exactly that. To browse for a book, follow these steps:

1   Click the **Subjects** button, highlighted next.

2   This should show a list of subjects you can browse, like Thriller, Historical Fiction, and Technology. Depending on the library, the list of subjects may be quite long, so you may need to scroll down to see them all. Click a subject you want to browse (for example, Mystery).

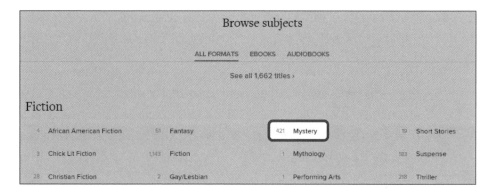

This should bring up a list of all the ebooks available from the library in that particular category, as shown next.

By default, OverDrive sorts the list by date added. You can sort this to show, for example, the most popular books first by clicking **Sorted by date added** and clicking **Popularity**, or you can choose another sorting option. You can also use the options in the filtering bar on the left side to narrow down the results. For example, click **Date added** and then **Last 14 days** to see only the books added in the last two weeks. Note that if the OverDrive window is too small, these options might appear in a drop-down menu titled "Filters" above the list of search results, rather than on the left side.

Click a book you're interested in to read more information about it.

BORROWING A BOOK

After you click a book, you should see a page with a description of the book as well as a list of similar books you might like. If the book is already on loan or you decide you don't want to borrow it, click the **back button** in the bottom-left corner to return to your search results. Make sure you don't click the back button in the top-left corner of the page, though, as this takes you all the way back to where you choose a library.

Once you've found a book you like, it's time to borrow it:

1   To borrow the book, click the **Borrow** button, highlighted next.

2   You may notice a drop-down arrow next to the Borrow button. Sometimes the library will give you the option of borrowing the book for a longer amount of time, and you can click the drop-down arrow to choose how long you'd like to keep it.

OverDrive should now confirm that you borrowed the book with an orange bar at the top of your screen.

DOWNLOADING A BOOK

Now that you have borrowed a book, you need to download it to be able to read it on your computer.

1   Notice that the Borrow button now reads "Go to Loans." Click **Go to Loans**, highlighted next, to see your loans page.

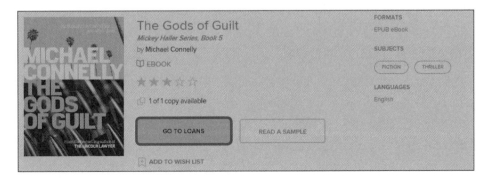

2 You should now see your loans page, which gives you a list of all the books you've borrowed from your library. Click the **Download** button underneath the book title, as highlighted next, to download the ebook onto your computer.

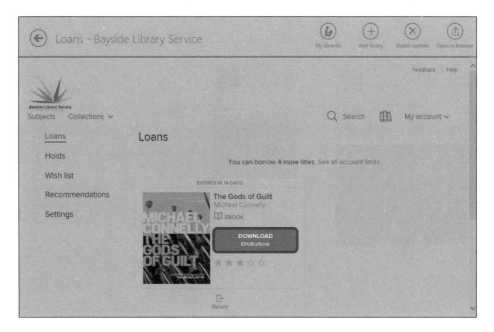

* **NOTE:** *Some books offer different download options, in which case your download button will have a drop-down arrow next to it. If that's the case, click the **drop-down arrow** and choose **EPUB eBook** from the list of options.*

3 You'll be asked whether you'd like to go to your OverDrive bookshelf or keep browsing for other books to borrow. Click **Go to bookshelf**.

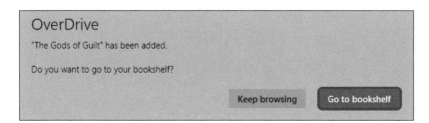

You should see the book you've just borrowed under the "Bookshelf" heading, as shown next. You can access your bookshelf at any time by clicking the **back button** in the top-left corner of the page.

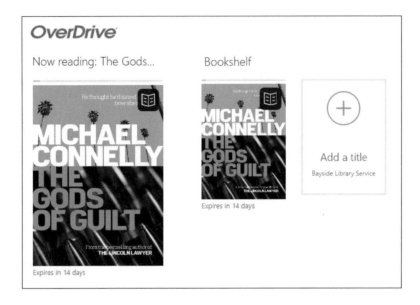

ACTIVITY #24

In this activity, you'll practice browsing through genres of ebooks and borrowing a book.

1. Use the browse feature to locate a book from your favorite genre.

2. Borrow the book you've found.

3. Download the book to your computer.

Reading a Book

Now that you've borrowed a book, it's time to read it! Follow these steps to read a book you borrowed:

1 From your bookshelf, click the book you want to read.

> ✱ **NOTE:** *If you haven't borrowed a book, your Bookshelf will appear empty, and you'll need to click* **Add a title** *and use the methods covered earlier to find, borrow, and download a book before continuing.*

2 This should open the book itself on your computer. Like with a paper book, you'll see the cover and then the preliminary pages first. You can flip back and forth through the pages by clicking the far left or far right side of the page. You can also use the left and right arrow keys on the keyboard to move between pages.

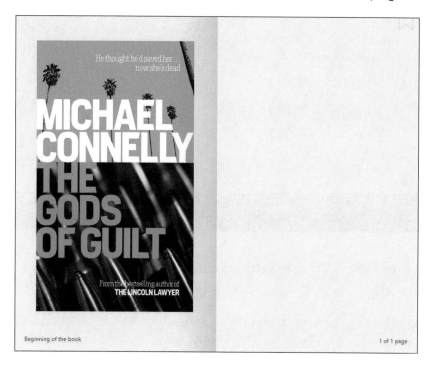

CHANGING THE FONT SIZE

If you find the font too small to read clearly, you can adjust it to make it bigger. To make the text larger (or smaller), follow these steps:

1 Click in the middle of the screen. This should bring up a variety of options on the top and bottom of the window.

2 Click the **Settings** button, highlighted next.

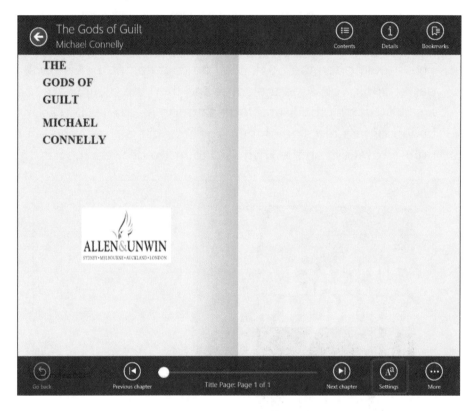

3 This should bring up a Settings screen on the right side of the page.

4 Click the drop-down box underneath "Font size" and choose a larger or smaller size. You should see the size of the text on the page change.

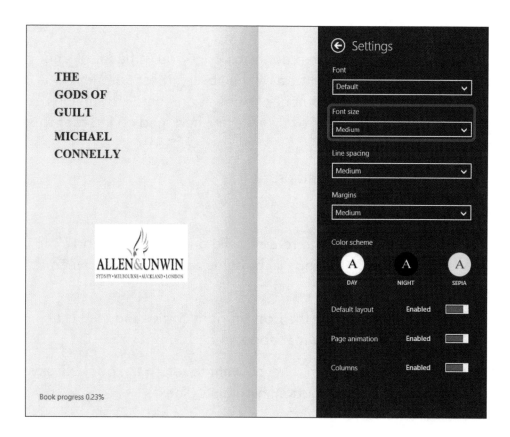

You might find some of these other settings useful as well. In particular, the "Color scheme" options let you change the page color and text color for the book. To return to the book after changing the settings, click anywhere on the book page.

CLOSING A BOOK

After you've finished reading the book, you can easily return to the OverDrive main page:

1 Click in the middle of the page.

2 Click the **back button** in the top-left corner.

You'll be returned to the OverDrive main page, and your place in the book will be automatically bookmarked. This means that when you open the book again, you'll be brought back to the last page you were reading.

RETURNING A BOOK

OverDrive automatically returns your book once you've had it for the maximum length of time permitted by the library. Most libraries also limit borrowing to a certain number of titles at one time. This means that you may want to return books you've finished reading in order to borrow more books.

To return a book, follow these steps:

1 Open your Bookshelf.

2 Click the book you want to return and then click in the middle of the book. This should bring up the same options you saw when changing the font size.

3 Click the **More** button in the bottom-right corner and then click **Delete/Return** in the list that appears.

4 You'll be asked to confirm that you want to return the book. Click the **Delete and return** button, highlighted next.

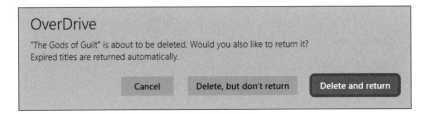

ACTIVITY #25

In this activity, you'll practice reading ebooks from OverDrive.

1. Open the book you borrowed in Activity #24.

2. Adjust the font size so that you can easily read the book.

3. Read the first few pages of the book you borrowed.

4. Return the book you just read.

Explore: Audiobooks

Some libraries complement their ebook offerings with a large selection of audiobooks. In OverDrive, audiobook listings will have the word *audiobook* under the author name rather than *ebook*. You can borrow and download audiobooks in exactly the same way as ebooks, and they will appear in your Bookshelf along with any ebooks you've borrowed. Provided you have speakers or headphones attached to your computer, you can listen to an audiobook by clicking it in your Bookshelf.

Phew, We Did It!

In this lesson, we looked at reading books for free online using the OverDrive app. You learned how to do the following:

✱ Browse and search for books on OverDrive

✱ Borrow ebooks from your local library using OverDrive

* Download and read ebooks on your computer

* Return an ebook on OverDrive

In the next lesson, you'll learn to stay in touch with friends and family using the free Skype app.

LESSON REVIEW

Congratulations! You've completed Lesson 10. Take this opportunity to review this lesson by completing the following tasks. If you can complete these tasks with confidence, you're ready for Lesson 11. If not, don't lose heart; just keep practicing!

1. Search for a book you like using OverDrive.

2. Browse your favorite book genre and borrow one you like.

3. Read and return the book you just borrowed.

LESSON 11
MAKING CALLS WITH SKYPE

Welcome to Skype! The Skype app lets you talk to your friends and family in real time on video, so you can see and hear them for free from anywhere in the world.

What Is Skype?

Skype is an app for communicating that gives you a way to make video or audio calls to your friends and family. It comes already installed on your Windows 10 computer and is free to use. It's similar to a telephone but with two huge advantages: you can see the person you're calling, and you can send written messages. For example, you can send happy-birthday notes, arrange lunch meetings, or even plan on a time to share a video call.

For Skype to work, both you and the person you want to contact need to have the Skype app on your computer. Fortunately, everyone with the latest version of Windows 10 will already have the Skype app installed. Millions of people around the world use Skype, so it's a very well-known app, and because it's free, a lot of people have it or can easily get it.

To talk to people on Skype, you first need to add them as contacts, and they need to add you; this helps protect Skype users against unwanted calls, calls from strangers, or scams.

Let's get started!

What Do I Need to Use Skype?

Skype runs through the internet, so you must have an internet connection to make a call or send a message. To make a call, you also need speakers and a microphone, and if you want to use video on your calls, you also need a *webcam* (a camera for your computer). All laptops and tablets will have these built in, and if you don't already have speakers, a microphone, and a webcam for your desktop computer, they are easily obtained from a local computer or electronics store.

Setting Up Skype

Let's open Skype and see what it's like. Skype is already installed on your computer, so you can open it from the Start menu in the exact same way you've opened apps in previous lessons.

1 Click the **start button** in the bottom-left corner of the screen and type **skype**.

2 Click **Skype** from the list that appears.

3 If this is the first time you've used Skype on your computer, you might be asked to sign in. Type in your Microsoft account (the same one you created in "Setting Up Your Computer" on page 17) and click **Next**, as shown below.

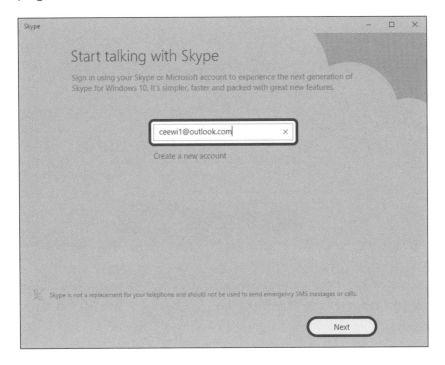

4 You'll then be asked to enter your password. This is the same password you use to sign in to your computer. Type it into the Password box and click **Sign in**.

5 If you haven't already provided your name to Microsoft, you may be asked to enter it now. This helps other people know who you are on Skype and is quite safe to do. Type your name into the **First name** and **Last name** boxes as shown here, and then click the **Next** button.

6 You might be asked to add friends and family as contacts. We'll look at doing this a little later, so for now click the **I'll do this later** button.

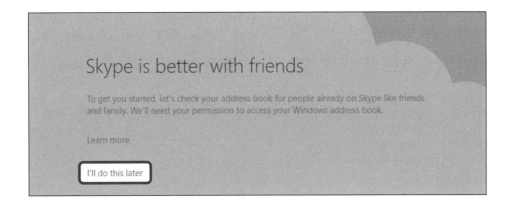

Skype is better with friends

To get you started, let's check your address book for people already on Skype like friends and family. We'll need your permission to access your Windows address book.

Learn more

I'll do this later

7 You might also be asked to add your phone number to Skype. This will allow people who know your phone number to use it to look you up on Skype, but don't worry—your number won't be visible to the general public. If you'd like people to be able to do this, enter your number and click **Next**. If you'd prefer not to provide this information, it is optional, so you can simply click **I'll do this later** instead.

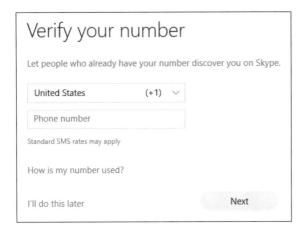

Verify your number

Let people who already have your number discover you on Skype.

United States	(+1) ∨

Phone number

Standard SMS rates may apply

How is my number used?

I'll do this later   Next

8 Finally, you'll be told that Skype's all set. Click **Finish** to start using Skype.

You should now be able to see the main Skype screen, which will look something like this:

Contacts

Recent conversations　　*Contacts list*

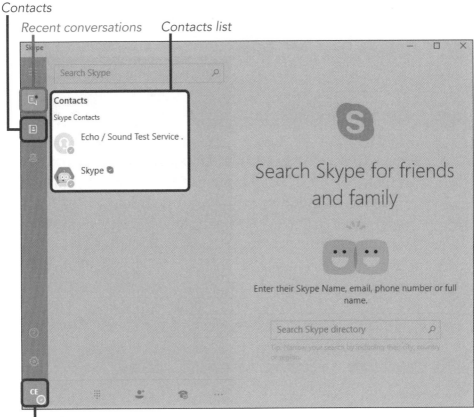

Profile

* **Contacts:** This button opens your contacts list. You'll learn how to add Skype contacts later in this lesson.

* **Recent conversations:** This button opens a list of your recent messages and calls.

* **Profile:** The circle icon with your initials in the bottom-left corner of the screen is the Profile button. Clicking this button opens the profile screen, which shows more information about your account.

Let's take a closer look at customizing your profile next.

ADDING A PROFILE PICTURE

Before you start making calls, it's a good idea to add a profile picture. This is a small picture that will appear when people try to find you and add you as a Skype contact. Adding a profile picture of yourself will make it easier for your friends and family to find the real you. If you're reluctant to add a picture of yourself, you can instead add a picture connected to your hobbies or interests. For example, you could use a picture of your dog!

To add a profile picture, follow these steps:

1 Click the **profile button**.

2 This will bring up your profile screen, which is where you can add information about yourself that other people can see. To use your webcam to take a picture to use as your profile picture, click the small **camera icon** below your initials, as shown next.

3 Your webcam will turn on, so you should now see the view from your webcam. If this is the first time you've used the webcam, you might be asked to give permission for Skype to do so. This is perfectly safe, so click **Allow** to proceed. Adjust your webcam or yourself so that you're in the middle of the frame. When you're happy with the shot, click the **camera icon**, highlighted next, to capture the image.

Manage Profile Picture

1.3M HD WebCam

Save   Cancel

If you like the photo, click the **Save** button. Otherwise, click the **trash can icon** to delete the photo and then click the **camera icon** again to take another photo.

4 You can also click the three dots between the camera and trash can icons to choose a picture from your computer to use as your profile picture instead of taking one with the webcam.

You should now be able to see your profile picture in place of your initials in the profile button, like so:

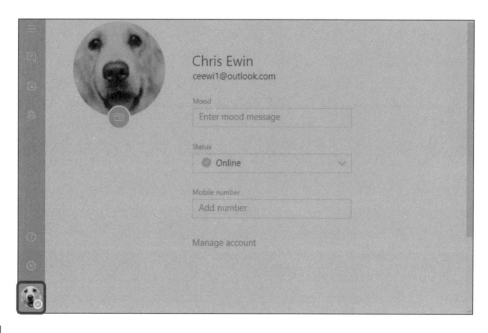

Chris Ewin
ceewi1@outlook.com

Mood
Enter mood message

Status
Online

Mobile number
Add number

Manage account

ADDING FRIENDS AS SKYPE CONTACTS

To contact someone on Skype, you need to add them as a contact. You can request that a friend or family member become your contact, and then they must accept your request before you can call or message them. If you've put contacts into your email address book in the past, you might find them showing up here in Skype as well. Don't be alarmed if that's the case.

Some people have their accounts set up so that anyone can call them without adding them as a contact, but in any case, it's polite to add someone as a contact before calling them. Once they're added, they'll appear in your list of contacts, which will make it much easier to talk to them in the future.

You can add a contact by searching for their profile using their name, email address, or cell phone number, if they chose to provide it. Searching for someone using their email address is usually more accurate because an email address has to be unique, while many people can have the same name. But if you don't know someone's email address, you can search for their name and use their profile picture to try to identify them. Alternatively, if your contact has an account that they created many years ago before Microsoft purchased Skype, they may have a different username known as a *Skype Name* that you can also use to find them.

Here's how to add someone as a contact:

1 Click the **contacts button** on the left side of the screen.

2 Click in the **Search Skype** box at the top of the page, shown here, and enter the name, phone number, or email address of a friend or family member who uses Skype.

3 A list of matching contacts and their profile pictures should automatically appear below the search box. If the person made their location public, you can see it below their name. Or, if you share any mutual contacts with the person, you'll see that below their name instead. *Mutual contacts* are Skype contacts that you and another Skype user have in common. This is particularly useful information as you're far more likely to know people with whom you share contacts.

4 Find the person you're looking for and click their name.

5 Click the **Add to Contacts** button on the right side of the page.

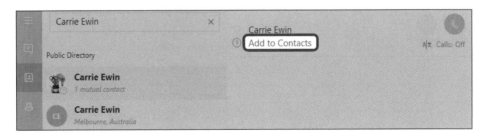

The person you've added should now appear in your contacts list, even if they haven't yet accepted your contact request. A small gray question mark will appear in the person's profile picture, highlighted next, to indicate that your request hasn't yet been accepted. When this disappears, it means they accepted your request, and you can call them.

ACTIVITY #26

In this activity, you'll practice adding someone to your list of contacts. Try adding one or two friends who use Skype to your contacts list.

ACCEPTING A CONTACT REQUEST

If someone adds you as a contact, you have the choice of accepting the contact request and communicating or refusing the request. If you refuse the request, don't fear—they won't be informed!

If you've received a contact request, a small red dot will appear beside the **Recent conversations** button on the left side of the screen. This tells you that you have unanswered messages or requests. You'll also see a box pop up in the bottom-right area of the screen telling you that you received a message, though this will disappear in a few seconds. The following figure shows both of these notifications.

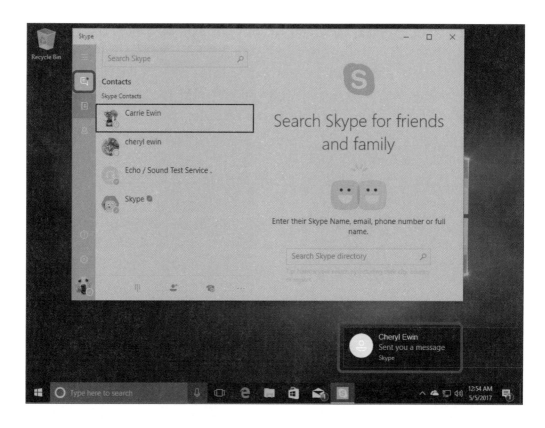

To answer a contact request, follow these steps:

1 Click the **recent conversations button**, which now shows a small red dot, to see any unanswered messages.

2 In this example, Cheryl Ewin has sent me one message.

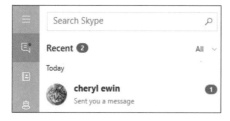

3 Click the name of the person who has sent the contact request.

4 This shows you their message and gives you the option to accept or deny their request.

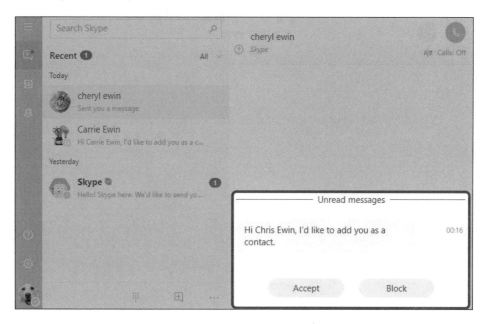

5 Click the **Accept** button. If you don't want this person to be able to contact you on Skype, you can click the **Block** button instead. This will prevent them from being able to contact you in the future.

If you accept the request, the section where the Accept and Block buttons appeared will now change to allow you to send a message to that person.

ACTIVITY #27

In this activity, you'll accept a contact request:

1. Ask a friend to add you as a contact on Skype.

2. Accept their contact request when it arrives.

Let's Start Calling!

Once you have people in your contacts list, you can start calling them. In this section, you'll learn to place an audio call, make a video call, and send written messages to your contacts.

AUDIO CALLS

An audio call on Skype is just like a phone call: you will be able to hear the other person but not see them. Let's try it out.

Making an Audio Call

To make a call that's just audio (no video), follow these steps:

1 Click the **contacts button** on the left side of the screen to open the contacts list.

2 Click the name of the person you want to call.

3 Click the **call button** at the top right of the screen, highlighted next.

A box will pop up on your contact's screen telling them that you're calling. Once they accept the call, you will be able to hear the other person, and they will hear you! If they're not at their computer or they don't answer the call, you'll simply be told "Call Ended."

The Audio Call Screen

If the call has connected you with your contact, you'll see a screen like the one shown here.

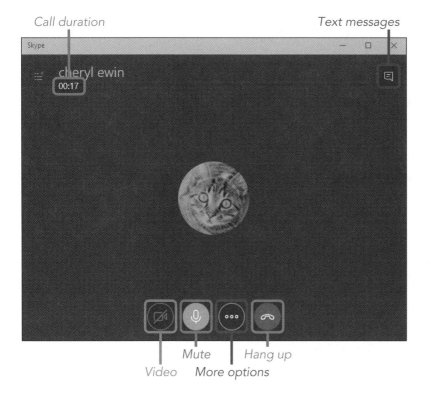

- **Call duration:** This tells you the length of your call.

- **Text messages:** This lets you type and send text messages to the contact while you're talking. This can be handy if you want to send something that's difficult to say accurately, like a long web address.

* **Video:** This turns your webcam on and off so you can control whether people can see you. It also turns your audio call into a video call, which we'll explore in the next section.

* **Mute:** This turns off your microphone so that the other person can't hear you, but you will still be able to hear them. Great if you need to sneeze! Click it again to turn the microphone back on.

   * *NOTE: If you find the volume is too low or too high to hear the other person properly, you can adjust it using the volume icon in the system tray, located in the bottom-right corner of your screen. To adjust the volume, click the **volume icon** and then adjust the slider until the volume is suitable.*

* **More options:** This lets you access a few other options, such as adding a third person to the call. We won't cover this capability in this book, but we encourage you to explore it on your own.

* **Hang up:** This ends the call.

Once you've finished making your audio call, click the **hang up button** to return to the main Skype screen.

VIDEO CALLS

A video call lets you *see* the other person as well as speak to them—you need to have a webcam on your computer to make video calls. Be aware that the person on the other side can see you as well!

1 Click the **contacts button** on the left side of the screen.

2 Click the name of the person you want to call.

3 Click the **video call button** on the right side of the screen, highlighted next.

If the other person answers your call, you will then be able to see and hear the other person, and they will see and hear you. You will also see a small window of what your own camera shows in the bottom-right corner of the screen. This way, you can adjust your camera (or your hair!) if you need to.

ACTIVITY #28

In this activity, you'll practice making a video call. Use Skype to video-call a friend.

RESPONDING TO A CALL

Of course your friends and family will want to call you as well! If you receive a call, you'll hear a beeping sound (as long as you have your sound on), and a Skype message will pop up on your computer screen. Skype will need to be set up on your computer for you to receive a call, but you don't need to be currently using it. This means that you can play a game, use the internet, answer emails, or whatever else you want to do on your computer and still receive a Skype call.

Just as you can choose to call someone with audio only or video, a friend or family member can also make this choice when they call you. The good news is that you can answer the call with your choice of audio or video! This means that your contact can begin a video call and you can choose to answer with audio only on your end. You'll enjoy the benefits of seeing them through video while only answering with audio.

Here's how to answer a call:

1   When a Skype message appears telling you that you have an incoming call, click the **Audio** button to accept it as a voice call, or click the **Video** button to accept it as a video call, like in the next figure.

2 Your call will then connect, and you can talk away!

3 Of course, if you're busy, you can always decline the call by clicking the **Ignore** button.

SENDING WRITTEN MESSAGES

When people send messages through Skype, they are usually short, typed messages, similar to text messages on a mobile phone. These are handy to send if you want to leave a message for someone who isn't online so they can reply later. Just like calls, written messages on Skype are completely free. Here's how to send a message:

1 Click the **contacts button** on the left side of the screen.

2 Click the name of the person to whom you wish to send a message.

3 Click in the **Type a message** box at the bottom right, shown next.

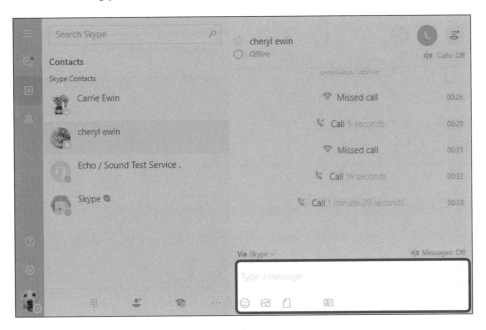

4 Type your message, and then press ENTER or click the blue button with the right-pointing arrow to send the message.

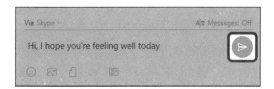

Your message should now appear on the right side of the screen, as shown here. This area is where all of your messages and previous Skype activity with that particular contact will be shown. When the other person replies, their message will appear here as well.

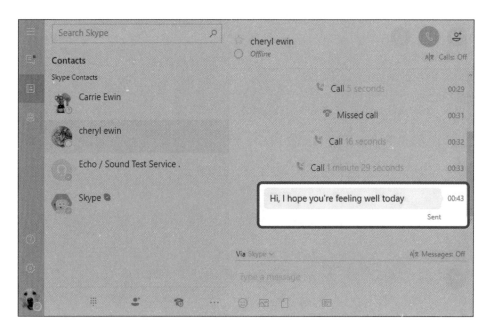

SENDING SMILEY FACES AND EMOTICONS

You can also send smiley faces or other little pictures known as *emoticons* along with your written message. These can be good to use to sum up a reaction you have to something someone said or just for a little fun! To send an emoticon, follow these steps:

1   Click the **emoticon button**, highlighted here, underneath the message box.

2 A pop-up box of emoticons, like the one shown here, will appear. Click an emoticon that you like.

3 The emoticon will appear as text in your message box, rather than as an image, as shown below. For example, the smiley face would appear as **:)**, whereas the love heart would appear as **(heart)**. Don't worry, though: it will show up as a picture once you send the message!

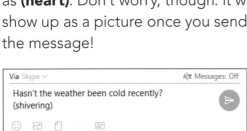

4 Press ENTER to send your message with the emoticon.

You should now see your message with an emoticon:

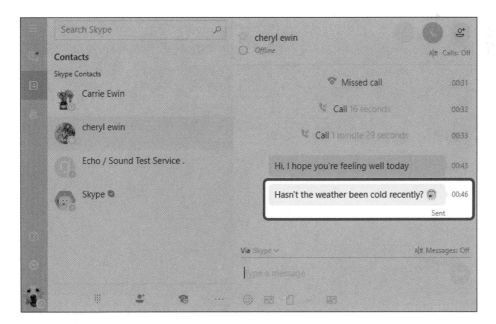

You can see new messages that people have sent you by clicking the **Recent conversations** button. The process is the same as receiving a contact request, so flip back to "Accepting a Contact Request" on page 227 if you're having trouble.

ACTIVITY #29

In this activity, you'll practice sending a written message to a friend.

1.   Send a text message to your friend.

2.   Once they've replied, send another message. This time, include an emoticon.

Deleting Skype Contacts

There may be times when you want to remove someone from your contacts list—perhaps you added the wrong person or you find you never interact with a particular contact using Skype. When you remove a contact, that person won't be notified, though if they're Skype savvy, they may notice a gray question mark next to your profile picture rather than your actual status, indicating that you are no longer a contact. To remove a contact, follow these steps:

1   Click the **contacts button** and then right-click the contact you want to remove.

2   A small menu will appear. Click **Remove From Contacts**.

That contact will then be removed from your contacts list. You won't be able to contact them, and they will need to send you another contact request in order to talk with you using Skype.

Staying Safe with Skype

Although Skype isn't as prone to security threats as email, there are still a couple of tips worth keeping in mind to stay safe while using Skype:

* Beware of accepting contact requests or responding to messages from people you don't know. They might be trying to scam you.

* Don't click links that your contacts have sent you if they come without any discussion or explanation. Your contact might have a virus on their computer that's sending out the link.

Phew, We Did It!

In this lesson, you learned to use Skype. You added people as contacts, made and received calls, and sent written messages. In this lesson, you learned how to do the following:

* Set up Skype on your computer

* Set up your profile, including adding a profile picture

* Add a person as a Skype contact

* Make an audio call

* Make a video call

* Send written messages, including emoticons

* Remove unwanted contacts

In the next lesson, you'll learn to create letters and documents using WordPad.

LESSON REVIEW

Congratulations! You've completed Lesson 11. Take this opportunity to review what you learned by completing the following tasks. If you can complete all of these tasks with confidence, then you are ready for Lesson 12. If not, don't lose heart—just keep practicing!

1. Open Skype.

2. Search for a friend and add them as a Skype contact.

3. Place an audio call to a friend using Skype.

4. Video-call a different friend using Skype.

5. Ask a friend to contact you at a predetermined time using Skype, and answer the call.

6. Send a friend a written message using Skype, including an emoticon.

LESSON 12
TYPING LETTERS AND DOCUMENTS

WordPad is a wonderful tool that you can use to create all kinds of documents, such as letters, invitations, and even posters.

In this lesson, you'll learn how to type up documents and how to change the color, size, and style of the text to customize your documents. You'll also learn to save the document so that you can find and edit it again later, and you'll learn how to print so you have physical copies of the document to pass out to your friends!

Why Use WordPad?

WordPad can help you create all different types of creative, attractive, basic, and professional-looking documents, including the following:

* Letters

* Reports

* Invitations

* Posters

* Cards

* Shopping lists

WordPad has many advantages over handwritten documents. Most importantly, typed letters are easier to read (especially for younger generations!), and if you make a mistake, you can simply delete your error and retype without making a mess. WordPad also lets you change the color, style, and size of your text as well as add pictures, which gives your document a professional look and tailors it to your needs. You can also save your document so you can revisit it at any time in the future.

WordPad is probably one of Microsoft's best-kept secrets. This helpful app is entirely free and simple to use to write documents. It certainly doesn't have all the bells and whistles of a full-fledged word processing program like Microsoft Word, but it does offer simplicity. Most importantly, WordPad is free, whereas Microsoft Word must be paid for. All the features of WordPad also exist in Microsoft Word, so if you're familiar with WordPad, you can easily get started with Microsoft Word as well. This means that WordPad is a great starting point, and if you find yourself wanting more, you can turn to Microsoft Word later.

Meeting WordPad

Like every other app, WordPad can be opened using any of the methods in the previous lessons. To open WordPad, follow these steps:

1   Click the **start button** in the bottom-left corner of the screen and type **wordpad**.

2   Click **WordPad** from the list that appears.

WordPad will open and will automatically create a new blank document.

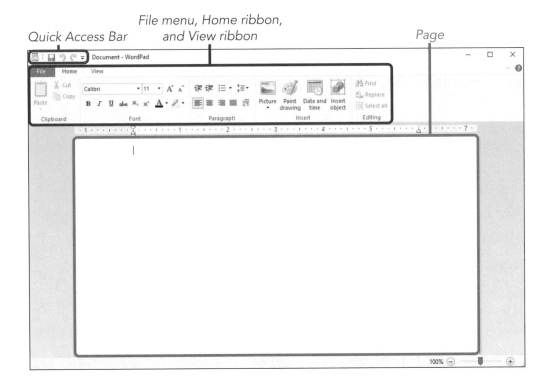

WordPad has a lot of features, so it's important to get comfortable with where to find things. The tools and buttons appear at the top of the screen. They're organized into a File menu, a Quick Access Bar, and two ribbons that contain the Home tools and View tools. Let's take a look at WordPad's features.

* **Quick Access Bar:** The Quick Access Bar provides a selection of the most useful tools in WordPad. These tools stay on the screen permanently. These are shortcuts to tools you can find in other ribbons. By default, the Quick Access Bar has tools to let you quickly save your document, undo a mistake you've just made, and redo that change if you then decide it wasn't a mistake after all.

* **Home ribbon:** The Home ribbon contains tools needed to create and change the appearance of your document. This includes tools for changing the size, color, alignment, and font of your text, and tools for adding pictures, drawings, and dates.

* **View ribbon:** The View ribbon holds tools that change the way you *see* your document. For example, from the View ribbon, you can zoom to make your document appear larger or smaller. This doesn't actually affect any of the text in your document, just how it appears on your screen.

* **File menu:** The File menu appears as a menu that drops down on your screen. It holds tools that let you work with your document as a whole. For example, after you've finished creating a letter, the File menu will help you save, print, or email the letter. The File menu also lets you open previously created documents, create new documents, and find out more about WordPad.

* **The page:** WordPad provides a fresh piece of white "paper" for you to write on. You'll find this page of "paper" in the middle of the screen.

ACTIVITY #30

Let's see if you've become familiar with the layout of WordPad! For this activity, find the tools that allow you to perform the following actions. You don't need to be able to do them just yet (you'll learn that later in this lesson). For now, just see if you know where to find things.

* Change the color of your text.

* Zoom in on your document so it appears larger.

* Print your document.

* Insert a picture into your document.

* Undo a mistake.

Typing Your First Document

You've opened WordPad, and you're now ready to begin creating your first document! Just like with a handwritten letter, you start a document by putting words on the page. You should see the cursor, a small flashing black line on your page. It shows you where the text will appear as you type.

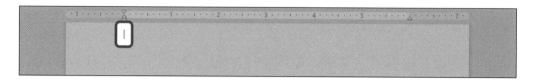

Use any letter key on your keyboard to type a few letters. If you hold down a letter key, you should notice that it repeats itself across the entire line and then moves onto the line below until you release it again. The automatic move to the next line is known as *word wrap* and is the hallmark of any word processing program. This means that you can concentrate on typing, and WordPad will move your text to the next line when required.

ACTIVITY #31

In this activity, you'll practice typing in your document. But first, let's start with a blank page. If you have any text on your screen, click at the end of the text and hold down the BACKSPACE key to delete it (see "The Keyboard" on page 16 for a key symbol diagram).

1. Type the sentence **WordPad is a very good program!!!**

2. Use the BACKSPACE key to remove all but the first exclamation mark.

Fixing Mistakes in Your Document

If you want to delete or add text, you will need to move the cursor to the point in the document where you want to make a change. Let's say you want to change "very good" to "great" in the sentence from Activity #37. Follow these steps to do just that:

1. Click after the word *good* in your document. You should see the cursor move to the point where you clicked. You can also use the arrow keys on the keyboard to move the cursor.

2. Use the BACKSPACE key to delete the words *very good*.

3. Type the word **great**.

4. Click at the end of the sentence to place your cursor there and continue writing your document.

Formatting Your Document

Currently, your document is looking quite plain. We want to liven it up with bigger text, colorful words, different text styles, and much, much more! This is known as *formatting* your document.

Before you can apply any formatting to your text, you must first *highlight* it. This means selecting the text so you can format it. Follow these steps to highlight text:

1. Click just in front of the text you want to select.

2. Hold down the left mouse button and keep it held down.

3. Drag the mouse to the end of the text you wish to select. Make sure to keep your mouse steady; if you drag it too far up or down, it will highlight the whole line. If you do highlight the wrong text, click elsewhere in the document to release the highlight and then try again.

4. Let go of the mouse button.

For example, here's how to highlight the word *great*:

1   Click before the letter *g*.

2   Hold down the left mouse button.

3   Drag the mouse to the end of the letter *t*.

4   Let go of the mouse button.

Highlighted text should appear as follows:

WordPad is a great program!

TEXT FORMATTING

Once your text has been highlighted, you can change its size, color, and style. You'll apply any of these text-formatting features using the Font box on the Home ribbon, highlighted next.

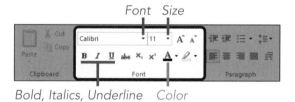

Font   Size

Bold, Italics, Underline   Color

Let's have a look at what these tools do and how to use them.

Changing the Font

The style of your text is known as the *font*. There are many different types of fonts—from traditional *script* styles to fun **chunky** styles. To change the font of your text, follow these steps:

1   Make sure you've highlighted the text you want to format (see the preceding section on selecting text).

2 Click the arrow in the box with the name of the current font.

3 Click the name of another font from the list that appears.

The font of only your highlighted text will change.

Changing the Size

Your text can also be made larger or smaller. Once again, highlight a word or a few words and then follow these steps:

1 Click the arrow next to the current size.

2 Click a different size. Larger numbers provide larger font sizes.

Changing the Color

The color of your text can also be changed. To do this, highlight a word and then follow these steps:

1 Click the arrow next to the selected color.

2 Click a new color from the list that appears.

Bold, Italics, and Underline

Bold, italics, and underline are three common ways of emphasizing particular words or sentences. To use them, highlight some text and select one of the following buttons:

* **Bold** B : Makes the text **thicker**.

* **Italics** *I* : Places the text on a *slant*.

* **Underline** U : Underlines the selected text.

In all cases, you can highlight the text again and click the same button a second time to return the text to normal.

ACTIVITY #32

In this activity, you'll practice using the text-formatting tools by changing the size and color of your text.

1. Underline the word *WordPad*. Remember to highlight the word first.

2. Change the font size of your entire sentence to 16. Remember to deselect the word *WordPad* by clicking elsewhere on the screen before highlighting the sentence.

3. Change the font color of your entire sentence to blue.

PARAGRAPH FORMATTING

The paragraph-formatting tools let you adjust the alignment of an entire paragraph of text. A new paragraph is begun when you press ENTER at the end of an existing paragraph.

1 Click anywhere in the paragraph you would like to adjust. Make sure the cursor has moved to somewhere within the paragraph. You don't have to highlight any text this time.

2 The paragraph-formatting buttons are in the Paragraph box in the Home ribbon, highlighted here.

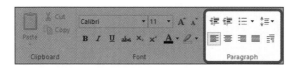

3 Click one of these buttons to format the paragraph as a whole.

There are the paragraph alignment buttons you can use:

* **Left align** ▤ : Aligns your text to the left of the page. This is the default alignment of text in your document.

* **Center align** ▤ : Aligns your text in the center of the page.

* **Right align** ▤ : Aligns your text to the right of the page.

* **Justify** ▤ : Aligns your text like newspaper print—fitting it from the left of the page to the right of the page and automatically adjusting the spacing so both edges are straight. You need at least one complete line of text; otherwise, it works the same as left align!

You'll notice some other formatting features within the Paragraph box as well. We won't cover them here, because they tend to be used less often, but we encourage you to explore these features on your own.

ACTIVITY #33

In this activity, you'll practice positioning paragraphs.

1. Create a new paragraph at the beginning of your document.

2. Type the heading **My First Document**.

3. Highlight the heading and increase the size of the font to 24.

4. Center the heading.

5. Start a new paragraph below the heading and then type today's date.

6. Right-align the date.

Undoing a Mistake

Undoing is an extremely helpful feature that lets you go back a step if you have made a mistake. If, for example, you italicized the wrong word and want to unitalicize it, instead of highlighting the word again and clicking the italics button, you can just click the **undo button** 🔄 in the Quick Access Ribbon. If you've accidentally undone something you wanted to keep, click the **redo button** ↪️.

Zooming In or Out

Zooming lets you magnify the text on the screen to make it easier to see. It does not affect the size of the text within the document, just how the document appears to you on the screen. To zoom in and out, follow these steps:

1 Find the zoom slider at the bottom right of the page.

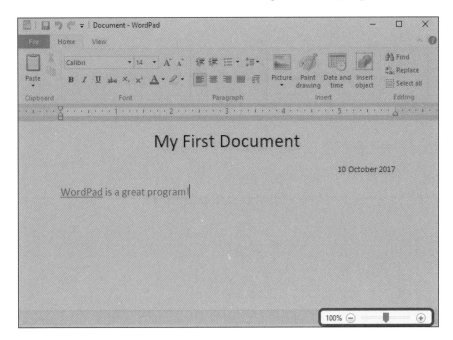

2 Click the ⊕ button to zoom in.

3 Click the ⊖ button to zoom out.

Saving Your Document

Saving a document lets you come back to it in the future, to look at the document or continue working on it. To save a document, follow these steps:

1   Click the **File** menu in the top-left corner of the screen.

2   Click the **Save** button from the list that appears. If this is your first time saving the document, WordPad will bring up the screen shown on the next page. This lets you choose where you want to save the document on your computer and what you want to call it.

> **✱ NOTE:** *By default, your document will be saved to the* Documents *folder. In Lesson 13, you'll see how to save the document to a different spot on your computer, but for now, let's just save it in the* Documents *folder and focus on the file's name.*

3   Click in the **File name** box. The text should all be highlighted in blue; if it isn't, highlight it with the click-and-drag mouse method discussed earlier.

4   Type **My First Document** as the file's name. This name will let you identify the document when you need to find it again.

5   Click **Save**.

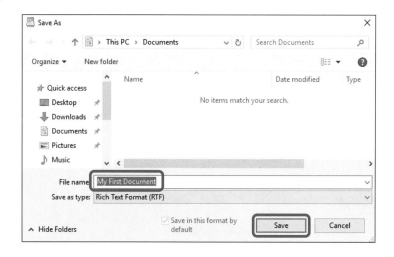

In the future, when you click the Save button for this document, this dialog will not appear again. WordPad remembers what you named the document and where you saved it and just replaces the old version with your latest version. But you still have to remember to save your document the first time—it won't save on its own! We'll see how to find the document and reopen it in the Lesson 13.

Printing Your Document

Printing a document requires that you have a printer installed. If you need advice on setting up a printer, check out "Connecting a Printer, Scanner, Webcam, or Other Device" on page 293.

To print a document, follow these steps:

1 Click the **File** menu in the top-left corner of the screen.

2 Click the **Print** button from the menu that appears. This will open the Print dialog.

3 Make sure your printer is the one selected underneath the **Select Printer** heading.

4 Click the **Print** button.

Your document should now print. If it doesn't print, check the name and model of the printer on the printer itself, like you did in Lesson 3, and make sure it matches the one in the Select Printer area.

Phew, We Did It!

In this lesson, we looked at creating documents with WordPad. You learned how to type a document and format it to make it look exactly how you want. In this lesson, you learned how to do the following:

* Start a text document

* Use the WordPad ribbons

* Format text, including changing its size, color, and font

* Align paragraphs across the page

* Undo mistakes

* Zoom in and out of the document

* Save the document

* Print the document

In the next lesson, you'll learn how to organize your files so that you can easily find your documents and pictures.

LESSON REVIEW

Congratulations! You've completed Lesson 12. Take this opportunity to review what you've learned by completing the following tasks. If you can complete all of these tasks with confidence, you are ready for Lesson 13. If not, don't lose heart—just keep typing!

1. Open WordPad.

2. Type out a vegetable lasagna recipe.

3. Format the text to make the recipe look how you want it to.

4. Save the recipe into the default *Documents* folder.

5. Close the document.

6. Open WordPad again.

7. Type out a to-do list for the week. Include a heading in the center of the page.

8. Save the list in the *Documents* folder.

9. Try out some buttons to see how this document's text can be formatted as a list.

10. Close the document.

LESSON 13
FILES AND FOLDERS

Learn how to organize your computer!

A *file* is a piece of information saved on your computer. For example, every letter, document, photo, song, and video saved on your computer is an individual file. Just as you store your bills, CDs, and letters in a certain place at home, every file you save on your computer is stored in a folder. The icon for a folder looks similar to the manila folders sold at stationery stores, and they have a similar purpose. Generally, it's good practice to store files that have something in common together inside a folder. This makes it easier to find the particular file you want.

As you begin to master your computer, you'll find yourself creating more files and folders. You'll need an easy way to remember *where* you stored your files and *how* to find them again. *File management* is the art of organizing your files so that they can easily be found and retrieved.

Exploring File Explorer

When organizing files, you can think of your computer as a filing cabinet that contains all of your saved files, and they are all organized into folders. To locate a file, you need to open the cabinet, look in the right folder, and find the right file. Simple!

To begin your search, you must open the File Explorer window. This is where you start your navigation of the folders in your computer. Follow these steps to open the File Explorer.

1 Click the **File Explorer** icon in the taskbar at the bottom of your desktop screen, as shown here. If you don't see the File Explorer icon in the taskbar, you can access it by clicking the start button, where you will find the File Explorer icon in the list on the left side.

2 The File Explorer window will then appear, showing you the **Quick Access** folder. This handy folder shows you the folders you use most often. Folder shortcuts in *Quick Access* will disappear if you don't use them regularly so as to keep only your most commonly used folders at hand.

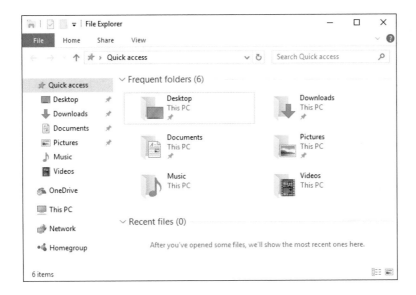

3 To find other folders that don't appear in *Quick Access*, use the *This PC* folder. To open this folder, simply click **This PC** from the list on the left side of the File Explorer window, as shown below. This opens the list of folders stored in *This PC*.

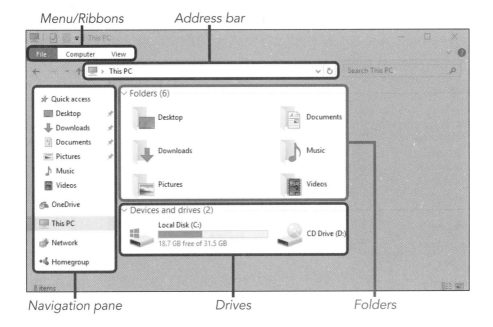

Menu/Ribbons   Address bar

Navigation pane   Drives   Folders

* **Menu/Ribbons:** Just like WordPad, a folder includes a set of useful ribbons with some of your most important buttons and tools. Inside the *This PC* folder, you have a Computer ribbon and a View ribbon. The contents of these ribbons are usually hidden to save space, and you can click the Computer or View button to display the ribbon. We'll look more at these ribbons and what they can do throughout this lesson.

* **The address bar:** This bar tells you which folder you're currently inside. In this example, we're inside *This PC*. The *Pictures* folder has its home inside *This PC*. If we opened *Pictures* to see some photos, the address bar would then show This PC▸Pictures. This lets us know that we're currently inside *Pictures*, which is inside *This PC*. The address bar will help you from getting lost!

* **The navigation pane:** The navigation pane appears on the left of the File Explorer window. This side section lets you see *all* the folders or locations on your computer, not just the handy folders you use often. We'll explore the navigation pane in more detail later in this lesson.

* **Drives:** A *drive* is a type of storage device that houses your folders and files. Your computer likely has the *C:* drive, which is a huge drive that stores almost everything on your computer. You can also get external storage devices, like USB flash drives, that you can plug into your computer and move files to and from. This gives you a way to transport files! We'll cover this topic later in the lesson.

* **Folders:** Your Windows computer will come with a number of useful folders already created to help you get started with the job of organizing your computer. Let's meet these folders:

    * **Desktop:** This folder shows you all of the items you've saved on your desktop.

    * **Documents:** Here you can store your text documents. In most cases, these will be the documents you create in WordPad. This might include letters, lists, reports, cards, budgets, invoices, or anything you want to type up.

    * **Downloads:** When you download documents, photos, or apps from the internet, the files will automatically be placed in the Downloads folder. You can move them to a different folder, but this is where there'll first appear by default.

    * **Music:** You can put all your favorite songs and audiobooks into this folder.

    * **Pictures:** You can store your photos and images in this folder.

    * **Videos:** You can put all your home movies or videos you download into this folder.

Opening a Folder

To find the files stored inside a folder, you first need to find and *open* that folder. A folder can be opened by double-clicking the folder icon.

1 Choose the folder you would like to open. In this example, we'll open **Pictures**, highlighted next.

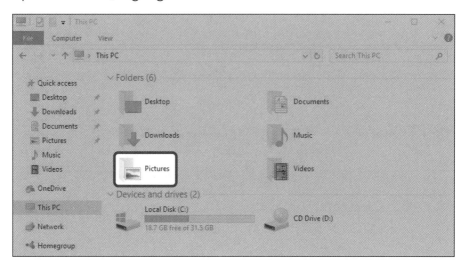

2 Double-click the folder icon.

3 The folder will then open, and you can see the files and folders inside. Remember you can use the address bar to work out exactly which folder you've opened.

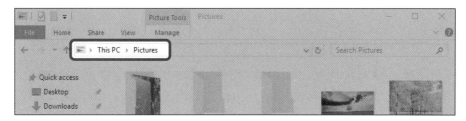

Over time, you may find you have created dozens of folders inside other folders, and it may take a while for you to click through to find the folder you want. Opening folders via the navigation pane makes it quick to open *any* folder on the computer, however deeply it's buried. Although it is a little trickier, it is well worth the effort. Follow these steps to open a folder from the navigation pane:

1 Open the File Explorer window if it's not already open. Remember that the navigation pane is located on the left side of the window.

2 Hover your mouse over any folder in the navigation pane, and a small triangle icon should appear to the left of the folder. This indicates that there are more folders inside this folder. (A folder inside another folder is known as a *subfolder*.)

3 Click the small triangle icon next to the folder—in this case, next to *This PC*—and the long list of folders inside will appear, as shown next. You might notice that the subfolders do not neatly line up underneath but instead are pushed slightly further to the right. This is a quick and easy way of showing that they're subfolders.

4 To open the folder, just click once on the folder's icon from the list that appears.

5 The folder will then open. Once the folder is opened, the triangle icon will change to point downward. Click this icon to close the folder, and all the subfolders will disappear from view.

Congratulations! You can now open and view any folder on your computer.

ACTIVITY #34

In this activity, you'll practice using File Explorer to find a file.

1. Return to *This PC*.

2. Open the *Documents* folder.

You should see the file *My First Document*, which we created in Lesson 12.

Working with Files and Folders

Once you've opened a folder, you'll need to be able to view and open the files inside it.

VIEWING FILES WITHIN A FOLDER

The icons for the files inside your folder may appear as little images that can be quite difficult to see. You can change the folder view so that the icons appear bigger or smaller, and sometimes show a preview of your document or picture. To change the view, follow these steps:

1 Make sure that you have a folder open.

2 Click **View** at the top of the File Explorer window. This will open the View ribbon.

3 The viewing options will then appear, as shown next.

Let's explore these options:

* **Extra large, Large, and Medium icons:** These views provide three sizes of icons. For photos and pictures, these views give you a preview of the image.

* **Small icons and List:** These views make your icons appear smaller but also help fit many more files onto the screen. Photos and videos show a generic icon rather than a preview of the image. This is ideal if you want to quickly browse a long list.

* **Details:** This view shows you more information about your files, such as the date the files were made and what type of files they are. This is very useful if you need more information to find a particular file.

264

OPENING A FILE

Once you've found the files you need, you'll want to open them. This way, you can check content, work on them some more, and share them.

1 Open a folder that has a useful file inside. In this example, we'll open *Documents* in *This PC*.

2 Find the file that you would like to view or open, such as *My First Document*, highlighted next.

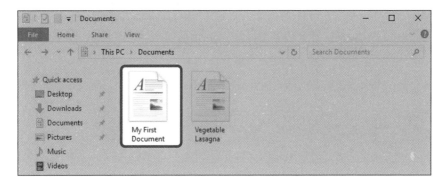

3 Double-click the file icon to open the file.

CREATING NEW FOLDERS

Now, to truly get organized, you'll learn to create brand-new folders that can contain new documents, photos, songs, videos, and more. Remember that your computer already has a useful selection of folders for these types of files: *Documents*, *Pictures*, *Music*, and *Videos*. We don't want to reinvent the wheel, so we're just going to create new folders inside these existing folders to help us organize our files further.

For example, maybe you're an avid cook and have a whole host of recipes. Because you're organized, you would like your recipes sorted into different folders according to the type of dish. This way, when you want to bake your famous chocolate cake, you can pull out your recipe in no time at all. In the following example, you'll create a folder called *Cake Recipes*.

1 Open the folder you want to create your new folder inside. In our example, we'll create the *Cake Recipes* folder inside the *Documents* folder, so go ahead and open **Documents**.

2 Once inside *Documents*, click the **Home** ribbon, highlighted next.

3 Click the **New folder** button inside the Home ribbon.

4 A new folder will appear with the rather dull name "New folder."

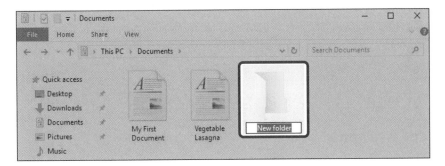

5 The folder's name should be highlighted in blue, indicating that you can simply begin typing a new name. If you accidently click somewhere in the name, the text will no longer be highlighted in blue. In this case, you can simply move the cursor to the end of the name and press BACKSPACE until all the letters are deleted; then you can begin typing.

✳ NOTE: *If you accidentally click somewhere else on the screen and you can't see the cursor inside the folder name, see "Renaming a File or Folder" on page 268.*

6 Type the new name **Cake Recipes**.

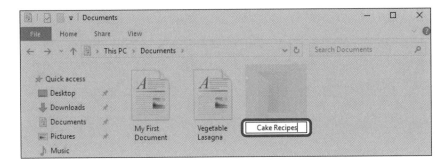

7 Press ENTER.

Your new folder has now been created!

RENAMING A FILE OR FOLDER

You can rename a file even after it has been created. For example, you might need to rename a file if you make a spelling mistake or realize the name is unclear. You can rename a folder in exactly the same way as you rename a file.

1 Click the file or folder that you want to rename.

2 Click the **Home** ribbon.

3 Click **Rename**, highlighted next.

4 The file or folder name should now be highlighted in blue.

5 Type the new name and press ENTER.

The file or folder will now be renamed!

DELETING A FILE OR FOLDER

Deleting a file will move it to the Recycle Bin, helping you keep your computer organized. You can delete a folder in exactly the same way as you delete a file. If you delete a folder, however, all of the files inside it will be deleted as well.

1 Click the file or folder you want to delete.

2 Click the **Home** ribbon.

3 Click **Delete**, highlighted next.

The file or folder will now be moved to the Recycle Bin.

RESTORING A DELETED FILE OR FOLDER

If you accidently delete a file or folder or just decide you want it back, you can go to the Recycle Bin and restore it.

1 Open the **Recycle Bin** from your desktop—you can get to the desktop by minimizing or closing all the files, folders, and apps you have open.

2 Find your file or folder (if you've deleted a lot of items, you might need to scroll through a bit) and then click it.

3 Click the **Manage** ribbon and then click **Restore the selected items**.

Your file or folder will then return to the folder you deleted it from!

ACTIVITY #35

In this activity, you'll practice creating, renaming, deleting, and restoring a folder using File Explorer.

1. Open the *Documents* folder.

2. Create a new folder called *Curry Recipes*.

3. Rename the folder to *Lasagna Recipes*.

4. Delete the *Lasagna Recipes* folder.

5. Go to the Recycle Bin and restore the folder.

Organizing Your Files

Now that you have some files and folders to work with, we'll look at some ways to keep your computer organized.

SAVING FILES INTO FOLDERS

The quickest way to stay organized is to save a file directly into the folder you want it stored in. In this example, we'll use WordPad to create a recipe that can be saved directly into its recipe folder.

1 Open WordPad. Remember that you can open WordPad by clicking the start button and typing **WordPad**.

2 Type a brief chocolate cake recipe.

3 Click the **File** menu in the top-left corner of the screen. Click the **Save** button from the list that appears. This will bring up the same Save As box you saw in Lesson 12. This time, though, you want to save your recipe *directly* into the *Cake Recipes* folder.

4 Open the **Documents** folder.

5 Open the **Cake Recipes** folder by double-clicking the icon.

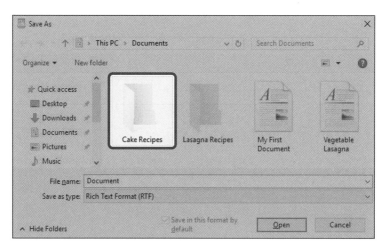

6 Your recipe will also need a name so that you can find it easily. Type **Chocolate Cake Recipe** into the File name box.

7 Click **Save**.

Congratulations! Your recipe has been saved to the *Cake Recipes* folder.

ACTIVITY #36

In this activity, you'll practice creating documents in WordPad and saving them directly into folders.

1. Open WordPad.

2. Type an apple cake recipe.

3. Save the recipe as a file called *Apple Cake* in the *Cake Recipes* folder.

MOVING FILES INTO FOLDERS

You may already have documents and images saved that you would like to organize. If you didn't save a file directly inside the folder you want, it's not too late! You can still move loose files into organized folders; for example, you might move a vegetable lasagna recipe file from *Documents* into a folder called *Lasagna Recipes*.

✱ **NOTE:** *In the following section, we will be working with the folder we created in Activity #41 and the recipe from the Lesson Review in Lesson 12. If you skipped those activities, it would be a good idea to go back to them now.*

Cut and paste is an excellent method for moving files into folders. The key idea is that you *cut* a file out of one spot and *paste* it into another, removing it from the first location. Think of it like cutting an article out of a newspaper and pasting it into a scrapbook.

1 Open the folder containing the file you want to move. In our example, this is the *Documents* folder.

2 Find and click the file. In our example, we will choose *Vegetable Lasagna*. A blue shading will appear once you click the file.

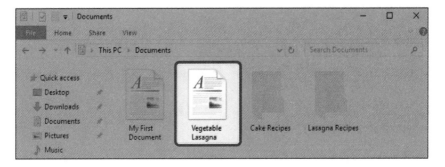

3 Click the **Home** ribbon.

4 Click the **Cut** button, highlighted next, which looks like a pair of scissors.

5 Notice that after the file has been cut, its icon will appear faded out. This is a sign that your cut has been successful!

6 Open the folder you would like to move the file to. In our example, we're moving the *Vegetable Lasagna* file into the *Lasagna Recipes* folder, so we'll open the **Lasagna Recipes** folder.

7 Inside the target folder, click the **Home** ribbon and click the **Paste** button, highlighted next, which looks like a clipboard.

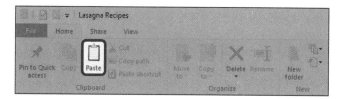

The *Vegetable Lasagna* file will now appear inside the *Lasagna Recipes* folder!

ACTIVITY #37

In this activity, you'll practice using the cut-and-paste method to move files around on your computer.

1. Open WordPad.

2. Create a *Meat Lasagna* file.

3. Save the recipe in the *Documents* folder and then close the document.

4. Open the *Documents* folder.

5. Cut the *Meat Lasagna* file and paste it into the *Lasagna Recipes* folder.

CLOSING A FOLDER

Closing a folder works in the same way as closing any document, app, or window. To close a folder, click the **close button** in the top-right corner of the folder. That window will now disappear.

Searching for Elusive Files

Understanding how files and folders are stored can give you a powerful sense of mastery over your computer! However, you may find that your files have been lost or forgotten and can be difficult to find. The Search box is an excellent solution—it will search through all areas on your computer for files or folders that match your search term.

1 Click in the **Search** box next to the Start menu, or simply click the **start button** itself.

2 Type the name of the file or folder you're searching for. If you're searching for a document and don't remember the name, you can search for a word or phrase you know is in the document.

3 Windows will offer a list of files and folders that match that search term, along with apps and even web results. Files will appear at the top of the list and will have a colorful icon to the left of the filename. Everything under the heading "Web" will perform a web search of your term.

4 Find your file and click it to open your missing file.

Taking Your Files on the Go

Your saved files aren't confined to your computer. There are several ways to move your files around, including emailing them as attachments, like you did with images in Lesson 4. You can also store them in a small portable memory device known as a USB flash drive, and even on the internet. There are lots of great reasons to keep a copy of your files in places other than just your computer:

* **To take files with you:** Often you'll want to be able to access your files from other computers. You might want to work on a document when you're on vacation, show photos to your friends and family at their homes, or have your photos professionally printed at a store.

* **For backup:** Storing your files only on your computer can be dangerous! If, for example, you are the victim of a robbery, your computer (and your precious files) could be taken and you'd lose them forever. Your computer might break down, or it could be attacked by a virus that deletes all your files. By storing your files in a second location, you have peace of mind knowing that no matter what happens, your files are safe.

STORING FILES ON A USB FLASH DRIVE

A *USB flash drive* is a portable stick with lots of room to store files. It's small enough to fit in your pocket but has enough digital space to store hundreds or thousands of files.

With the exception of some tablets, you can plug a USB flash drive into almost any type of computer *and* it doesn't require access to the internet. So whether you're traveling to Africa or Antarctica, your files can safely travel with you on your USB flash drive.

To stores files on a USB flash drive, the drive must be connected to the computer. Once the drive is connected, you can open it much like with any other folder on your computer. To connect and open a USB flash drive, follow these steps:

1 Find the right-sized connection (or hole!) on your computer (refer to the following figure). The connection should fit the USB flash drive, so it will be rectangular, and it might have the USB symbol: ⟳.

2 Plug the (usually silver) connector of the USB flash drive into the correct connection on the computer. It will only fit one way, so if you're having trouble connecting the drive, it might be upside down—or you might have the wrong hole!

3 Open **File Explorer** from the taskbar or Start menu.

4 Look at the navigation pane and you should see your flash drive, identified either by the brand name of the drive or simply as the rather generic "Removable Disk." Whatever it is called, it will be a new drive that wasn't on your computer before.

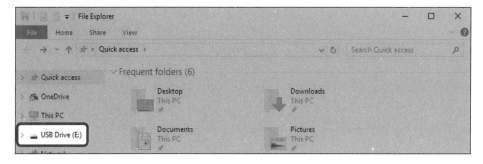

5 Click the USB flash drive to open it in the window.

6 The files and folders on your USB flash drive will then be displayed. If you've never used the drive before, it might not contain any files, in which case it will simply say "This folder is empty."

7 Double-click a file or folder to open that item on the USB flash drive. You can save these files to your computer, too, in the same ways you moved files earlier.

You can move files onto the USB flash drive using the cut-and-paste method. It's usually better to leave a copy of your files on your computer as well so that you don't lose your files if you lose your flash drive. You can do this by clicking the **Copy** button instead of the **Cut** button when moving your files.

ACTIVITY #38

This activity will give you a chance to practice copying files and folders to a USB flash drive. You can copy entire folders in the same way that you copy individual files.

1. Find the *Cake Recipes* folder. This folder contains many recipes you might want to take with you.

2. Copy and paste the folder onto your USB flash drive.

3. Open the USB flash drive folder. Locate the *Cake Recipes* folder that you added to the USB flash drive.

4. Open the *Cake Recipes* folder and view the recipes inside.

5. Close the USB flash drive folder.

STORING FILES REMOTELY WITH ONEDRIVE

OneDrive is a wonderful free app made by Microsoft that lets you store a copy of your files on the internet, a method of storing known as *cloud storage*. Storing your files in OneDrive allows you to access them from anywhere in the world (even on vacation!) as long as you have an internet connection, and it provides a storage space protected from physical disasters or theft.

OneDrive stores files on the internet, but the app makes your life easier by appearing as a folder on your computer. Although the files are actually *stored* on the internet, you can still *access* the files from the OneDrive folder on your computer, just like with any other folder. Neat!

Before you can use OneDrive, you need to set it up. Fortunately, this is very easy! Follow these steps to set up and open the OneDrive app.

1 Click the OneDrive icon, which looks like a pair of clouds, in the system tray.

2 If you don't see the OneDrive icon, click the Show Hidden Icons arrow in the system tray, as shown here. You should then see the icon in the box that appears.

3 If a message appears informing you that OneDrive is up-to-date, as shown here, then OneDrive has been set up on your computer. If not, follow the instructions on the screen to set up OneDrive.

4 Open **File Explorer**.

5 From the navigation pane, click **OneDrive**, highlighted next.

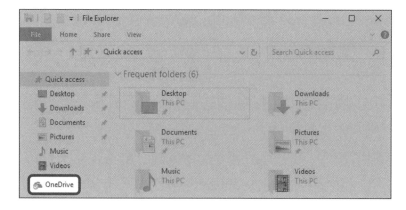

OneDrive will now open as a File Explorer window! The OneDrive folder works in exactly the same way as any other folder on your computer. You can move files into OneDrive using the copy-and-paste method, and files in OneDrive can be opened like any other file.

Explore: The OneDrive Website

The OneDrive website lets you access files you've placed into OneDrive from any computer in the world! To access the OneDrive website, open **Microsoft Edge** and enter **onedrive.live.com** into the address bar. Click **Sign in** and enter your Microsoft account details, and then you should see a page like the one below. It looks slightly different from the files and folders on your computer, but navigating them works in the same way.

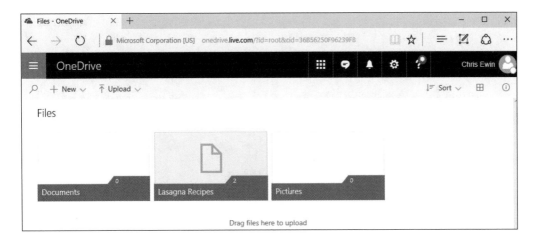

Phew, We Did It!

In this lesson, we looked at creating and organizing your files and folders. You learned how to do the following:

* Use File Explorer to find the files you've created

* Change the folder view to make icons larger or smaller

* Rename files and folders

* Delete and restore files

* Save files into folders

* Move files around using the cut-and-paste method

* Use the Search feature to find lost files

* Put files on a USB flash drive or in cloud storage

The next lesson is our final lesson! You'll learn all about staying safe on your computer and online.

LESSON REVIEW

Congratulations! You've completed Lesson 13. Take this opportunity to review what you've learned by completing the following tasks. If you can complete all these tasks with confidence, move on to Lesson 14. If not, just keep practicing with your files and folders!

1. Use WordPad to create a soup recipe and save it into the *Documents* folder.

2. Use File Explorer to create a new *Soup Recipes* folder.

3. Use the cut-and-paste method to move the soup recipe into the *Soup Recipes* folder.

4. Change the view to Large icons so you can clearly see each recipe's icon.

5. Use WordPad to create a second soup recipe. Save it directly into the *Soup Recipes* folder.

6. Plug a USB flash drive into your computer.

7. Copy the *Soup Recipes* folder to the USB flash drive.

LESSON 14

STAYING SAFE ONLINE

In our final lesson, we'll look at how you can protect yourself online and make sure your computer continues to run at its best in the future.

The purpose of this lesson is not to scare you away from using your computer, but to make you feel safe by letting you know the kinds of threats that are out there and how to protect against them. Once you know how to do that, you should feel much more confident!

Protecting Against Viruses

One of the greatest threats you can encounter on your computer is a *virus*, a malicious app or program whose purpose is to attack your computer. There are many different viruses that do many different things—from stealing your passwords and bank details to trying to convince you to buy fake apps for your computer. You might also have heard the terms *malware*, *trojan*, *spyware*, and *worm*, but we'll just call them all viruses. Luckily, there are things you can do to protect against the threat of viruses and to combat them if your computer gets infected.

RECOGNIZING THE SYMPTOMS OF A VIRUS

First, let's discuss how to recognize a virus when it strikes. Although far from an exhaustive list, here are some common signs of a virus:

* **Unexpected messages popping up on your computer, even when you're not browsing the internet:** Sometimes viruses will even appear as a fake app or website asking you to pay money to remove other viruses from your computer! Be wary of pop-up messages from sites or programs you don't recognize or trust.

* **Internet search results taking you to the wrong websites:** Some viruses will interfere with your search results, redirecting you to (often unsavory) websites.

* **Unexpected credit card charges or money missing from your bank account:** Sometimes you'll first find out that your computer has a virus via a phone call from the bank. Some viruses will try to steal credit card and bank details you've typed in on an infected computer.

* **Unexpected fake emails, Skype messages, or Facebook posts being sent from your computer to other people:** If your friends are telling you that they've received messages from you that you haven't sent, you might have a virus. Viruses sometimes spread themselves by sending out these sorts of messages, and some will even use these messages to ask your friends to send you money, when it's going to the virus creator.

* **Your computer is very slow or experiencing a lot of errors:** Some viruses will use your computer for their own purposes, slowing it down in the process. Of course, there are many, many reasons for a slow computer other than a virus, so don't jump to conclusions based off this one symptom alone.

Although this may sound scary, there are steps we can take to protect ourselves from viruses. Perhaps the most important tool available for staying safe online is an *antivirus app*, which will scan every file you open and every website you visit for signs of a virus. If it does find a virus or even suspects that something might be infected, it will prevent the program from running or the website from opening. An antivirus app can also scan your computer for viruses that are already present and remove any it finds.

Many antivirus apps are available, some for free and some you need to pay for. You might have heard of antivirus apps such as Norton and McAfee, but here we'll focus on Microsoft's Windows Defender app, which is free and comes with Windows 10. Even if you're using a different antivirus app, you can still run a scan with Windows Defender to give you a second opinion.

PERFORMING A SCAN WITH WINDOWS DEFENDER

To minimize the risk of getting a virus, Windows Defender automatically performs a complete scan of your computer at 2 AM each day. If your computer isn't turned on at 2 AM, it will reschedule the scan.

If you suspect that your computer might have a virus or if you just want to make doubly sure you're not infected, you can use Windows Defender to manually run a scan. Here are the steps to follow:

1 Click the **start button** in the bottom-left corner of the screen and type **defender**.

2 Click **Windows Defender Security Center** from the list that appears, as shown here.

3 You should now see the Windows Defender Security Center. The Windows Defender Security Center contains a number of useful features that you might like to explore on your own. We'll focus on the Virus & threat protection feature, which is responsible for protecting you from viruses. Click the **Virus & threat protection** button.

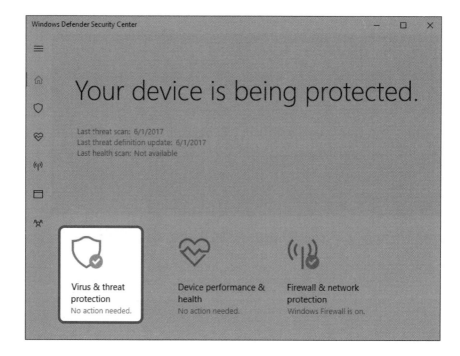

4 Click the **Quick scan** button, highlighted next.

✱ **NOTE:** *If you have another antivirus program installed on your computer, you might not see the "Quick scan" button. In that case, click the down arrow next to **Windows Defender Antivirus Options** and then click the **Periodic scanning** slider to turn it from Off to On.*

5 Your computer will now be scanned for viruses. This might take a few minutes depending on the speed of your computer and how many files you have on it.

6 Once the scan finishes, you'll be told the results, like in the following figure.

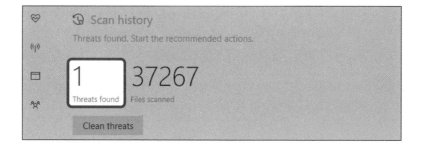

7 If any threats are found, Windows Defender will give you the option to remove them. Click the **Clean threats** button, highlighted next, to do so.

8 Windows Defender will remove the threats, which might take a few seconds. After it's finished, you'll be returned to the main Virus & threat protection screen.

If you're still having troubles after removing threats with Windows Defender, you can try running an Offline scan. This will take longer, and you won't be able to use your computer while it's running, but is more likely to remove any viruses that are present. To run an Offline scan, click the **Advanced scan** button, check the **Windows Defender Offline Scan** option, and choose **Scan now**.

HOW ELSE CAN I PROTECT MYSELF?

Even if you're using an antivirus app, a good way to protect yourself is to be careful with the sites you visit and the links you click. Here are some good strategies to protect yourself:

* Avoid clicking suspect ads on the internet. Some ads will tell you that you've won a prize, offer to help speed up your computer, or ask you to download an "important"' program. These links may contain viruses, and it's best to ignore them to be safe.

* Avoid visiting websites that promote illegal or suspicious activity, such as those promoting copyright infringement.

* If a message pops up telling you that your computer is infected, don't click it. It might be an ad trying to get you to install fake software, or even a virus trying to fool you into making the problem worse. Instead, look for a close button or Close link to close the message; then run a scan with Windows Defender or your trusted antivirus app.

* Never open attachments or click links in emails or Skype messages from people you don't know.

* Never open attachments or click links in emails or Skype messages from people you *do* know if you aren't expecting them, or if their message doesn't sound like them. If their computer is infected with a virus, it may be trying to spread onto yours through an infected email.

* Be careful with USB flash drives. If you plug a USB flash drive into a computer that's infected with a virus, it might spread onto the USB flash drive, which could then infect any other computer you plug it into. Only use flash drives on computers you trust.

* Avoid using banking websites or typing in credit card information on public computers like the ones at libraries or internet cafés, because they may contain viruses.

What Else Should I Be Aware Of?

The two other major threats on the internet are *scams* and *phishing*.

AVOIDING SCAMS

Internet scams often come in the form of emails offering you a great deal of money for doing practically nothing or asking you for quick money that will be returned with interest. An example of a scam email appears on the next page.

Dearly Beloved !!

to Karina

Feb 10 (12 days ago)

Dearly Beloved,

My name is Karina Alejo a dying woman who has decided to donate what I have to you/church. I am 69 years old; I was diagnosed with esophageal cancer 2 years after the death of my husband who has left me everything he owned. My doctors told me i will not live long because of my health, that is why i decided to WILL/donate my money to you for the good work of humanity, to help the motherless, less privilege and also for the assistance of the widows.

Here are the Contact details of my lawyer:
Name: Fabricio ERNESTO.
Email: fabricio.ernesto@aim.com

I have notified him about you. I know I don't know you but I have been directed to do this. I wish you all the best and may the good lord bless you abundantly, and please use the money well and always remember to extend the good work to others.

Yours in the Lord,

Karina Alejo.

This is just one example of a scam email. Others might say that you have won a lottery you never entered or have been named the sole heir to a deceased Nigerian prince, or they might ask you for money for some urgent situation with the promise that they will pay you back in full—and then some.

If you respond, you'll usually be told that all you need to do is send them a small amount of money to cover customs duties, processing, fees, or some other type of expense. The scammers will then extract as much money as they can out of you before moving on. If you ever receive one of these emails, it's best to delete it without responding, even if you have only the slightest suspicion that it's a scam.

AVOIDING PHISHING ATTACKS

Phishing attacks also usually come in the form of emails. In this attack, scammers typically send an email pretending to be from a legitimate company, like your bank, and try to get you to click a link in the email. That link will often take you to a website that's a near exact replica of the real bank's website, where they'll ask for your login details. If you hand them over, the scammers will likely drain your bank accounts! Phishing emails pretending to be from a bank are some of the most common, but scammers will also try to impersonate your internet service provider; popular sites like Facebook, Amazon, eBay, and PayPal; or even the IRS! Phishing attacks are generally subtler than other types of scams and thus harder to identify. Here are some tips that can help you identify a phishing email:

* **A generic greeting line such as "Dear Sir or Madam":** Real emails from banks and other sites usually address you by name.

* **An email address that doesn't match who the sender claims to be:** You would, for example, expect a real email from the Bank of America to come from an **@bankofamerica.com** email address. Therefore, if you receive an email from an **@gmail.com** address claiming to be from the Bank of America, it's probably a fake. Beware, though: it's not always so easy to spot the difference. A fake email from **@bankofannerica.com** might look at first glance like it's coming from the right place!

* **The wrong web address:** If you click a link in an email, you can check which website you've been taken to by looking at the address bar. If the address isn't what you expected, it could be a phishing email. The real Bank of America web address, for example, looks like this:

* **Poor spelling and grammar:** Many phishing emails are sent from countries where English isn't the primary language, so they often contain spelling and grammatical errors. Real companies usually proofread their emails, so any mistakes are a possible sign of a phishing email.

* **Urgent language:** Many phishing emails will try to pressure you into responding by including language such as "your account will be disabled if this isn't completed within 24 hours." A real bank probably wouldn't email you about something that important, but would phone you instead!

As with scam emails, if you do receive a phishing email, you should delete it without replying. Under no circumstances should you do as the email instructs. If you're unsure, try contacting the company the email claims to be coming from on the telephone and asking whether they sent it. We encourage you to take a look at *http://www.sonicwall.com/phishing/* as well, where you can take a quiz to test your ability to identify phishing emails, and learn more about phishing attacks.

> *✳ **NOTE:** You should never give any account passwords or bank or credit card information in an email. A bank would never ask you to email this information, so if an email asks you for it, it's almost certainly malicious!*

Getting Help

As our final lesson comes to an end, you should now have an excellent understanding of how to use your computer. But the journey doesn't end here! Your computer includes plenty of other useful features, and we encourage you to continue exploring all that your computer has to offer. As you do, you might find that you have new questions or need some help. Fortunately, Microsoft offers an excellent support center for this very reason. Microsoft Support has information on lots of topics and answers to common questions. To open Microsoft Support, follow these steps:

1   Open Microsoft Edge.

2   Type **support.microsoft.com** into the address bar. It will take you to the Microsoft Support page.

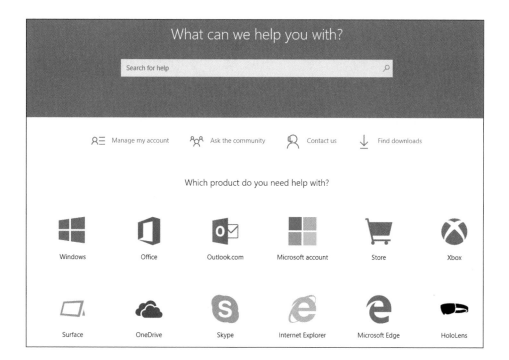

3   If you would like help on a particular topic (such as downloading apps from the Store), then type your question in the search bar and press ENTER. Your answer will appear!

4   If you're not quite sure what you would like to ask or would like more general Windows 10 information, you can click the Windows icon, highlighted here.

5   This will take you to the Windows 10 help page where you can find information, support, and answers to common questions.

Phew, We Did It!

In this lesson, we looked at security and troubleshooting. You learned how to protect yourself against and remove viruses, and how to avoid scams and phishing attacks. In this lesson, you learned how to do the following:

* Open Windows Defender

* Run a virus scan using Windows Defender

* Protect yourself against viruses, scams, and phishing attacks

* Get help with Microsoft Support

Thanks for reading this book! We hope you've enjoyed reading about using your computer as much as we've enjoyed writing about it. But don't stop now—keep on exploring your computer and finding new things to love! Best of luck!

LESSON REVIEW

Congratulations! You've completed Lesson 14. Take this time to review what you've learned by completing the following tasks.

1. Use the Microsoft Support page to find out how to organize your apps.

2. Look through your email inbox for any scams or phishing emails, and delete any you find.

CONNECTING A PRINTER, SCANNER, WEBCAM, OR OTHER DEVICE

Some tasks you do with a computer, such as printing and scanning, require an extra device. You'll need to connect this device to your computer to let them communicate and work together. Most modern printers, scanners, webcams, and other devices connect via a USB connection. With Windows 10, you can just plug in these devices and they're ready to go. However, you sometimes need to install a device so your computer can recognize it and what it does. We'll cover both scenarios here. Fortunately, the processes for installing different devices are very similar and fairly simple. However, if you do run into any trouble, make sure you consult your device's quick start guide—usually a pamphlet that comes with your device—for more details.

Connecting Your Device

To get your device working with your computer, you must first plug the USB cable from the device into a USB port on your computer. Here are the steps to follow:

1 If your device requires power, plug the power cord into a power outlet. The other end of the power cord should plug into a matching port somewhere on your device—most likely the back or bottom. Again, check the instructions for the device if you aren't sure.

2 If your device has a detachable USB cable, connect one end of the cable to your device.

3 Connect the rectangular end of the USB cable (shown on the right side of the image) to your computer in the correctly shaped hole. You might see a message pop up briefly in the bottom-right corner of your screen, such as the one shown here.

Most of the time, your device will then be ready to use, but sometimes you need to install an app to help it get going; we'll cover this next.

Installing Your Device

After you've connected your device, you need to help your computer recognize the device so they can communicate. To do this, you might need to install a *driver*, which is a simple type of software that lets the computer and the device speak the same language.

Fortunately, Windows automatically installs drivers for most devices as soon as you connect them to your computer, in which case you don't have to do anything. However, if Windows can't find the correct driver, you might need to find and add the driver yourself using a CD that came with the device. To check whether Windows has found the correct driver, try using your new device. If the device works, then it means Windows has found and installed the driver and you won't need to! If the device doesn't work, follow these steps to find and add the driver:

1 Insert the CD into your computer's CD-ROM drive with the label facing up. Your software installation should start automatically.

2 If it doesn't, open File Explorer as you did in Lesson 13, by clicking the **File Explorer** icon in the taskbar.

3 From the list on the left side of the File Explorer box, click **This PC**.

4 Double-click the **CD Drive** icon listed inside *This PC*. The name of the drive should change to reflect the CD you inserted.

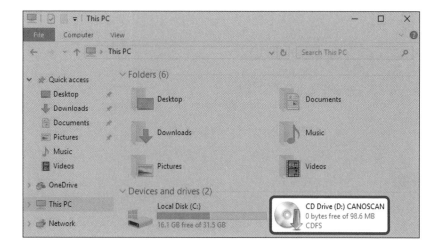

5 You may be asked to give permission for the driver to make changes to your computer. This is perfectly safe. Click **Yes**, highlighted next, to continue.

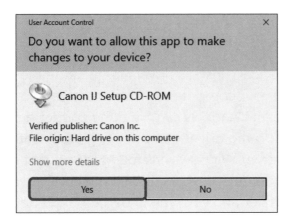

6 The setup process should now begin. From here, the process varies depending on your device and manufacturer, so do your best to answer the questions as prompted and click through the installation.

Once your device driver has been installed, you can begin using it. If your device still doesn't work, consult the device's user manual.

SWITCHING TO A MICROSOFT ACCOUNT

If you found that your computer was already set up without you having to go through the steps in "Setting Up Your Computer" on page 17, it's possible that you have a *local account* rather than a Microsoft account. This can happen if you upgraded from an older operating system, like Windows 7, or if the shop selling you the computer set it up in advance. A local account lets you log into your computer and use it in the same way, but it doesn't give you access to any of Microsoft's online services such as the Store, OneDrive, Skype, and the Mail app, which you'll need for this book. Here's how to check if you have a Microsoft account and, if you don't, how to create one.

Do I Have a Microsoft Account?

To check whether you have a Microsoft account or a local account, follow these steps:

1 Click the **start button** in the bottom-left corner of the screen.

2 Click the **settings button**, highlighted here.

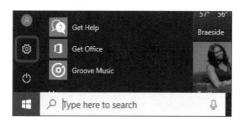

3 This should bring up the Settings screen. Click the **Accounts** option.

4 You should see a line of text underneath your name. If this line shows your email address, it means you have a Microsoft account and there's no need to proceed to set one up. If this line says "Local Account," you don't have a Microsoft account, so continue to the next section to create a Microsoft account.

Creating a Microsoft Account

If you have a local account, you'll need to switch to a Microsoft account to use all of the features available in Windows 10.

1 Click the **Sign in with a Microsoft account instead** link.

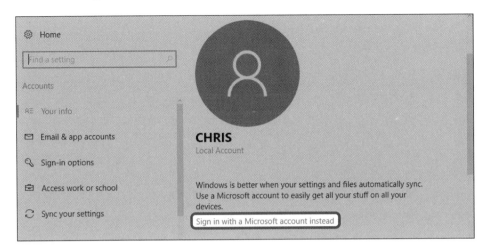

2 Follow the steps onscreen to create a Microsoft account. The process is very similar to "Creating a Microsoft Account" on page 20, so flip back for more information if you need help.

3 You will now be taken back to the Accounts screen in the Settings window, where you should be able to see your new Microsoft account.

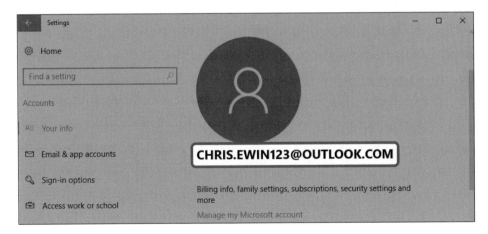

Now that you've created a Microsoft account, you're ready to work through all the chapters in the book in order to explore Windows 10.

CONNECTING TO WI-FI OUTSIDE YOUR HOME

You might have heard the term *free Wi-Fi* at a library, café, or hotel. This means that wireless internet access is being offered at no charge. If you have a laptop or tablet, you can connect to Wi-Fi using the following steps. You can also use the same process to connect to a friend or family member's wireless internet connection in their home—as long as they give you the password!

Follow these steps to connect to a free public Wi-Fi network:

1 At the bottom-right corner of your screen, you should see a little internet symbol that looks like the one highlighted here. Click this internet icon.

2 This should bring up a list of nearby wireless internet connections within range of your computer. Click the wireless connection you want to use.

3 Click the **Connect** button.

4 Type the password for this wireless internet connection, being careful to get the case precisely right. If you're at a café or a hotel, someone who works at the establishment should be able to provide you with the password.

5 Click the **Next** button.

You should now be connected. Once you are connected, the internet symbol will change to show you the signal strength, as you can see here. If you click the internet symbol again, you should also see the word *Connected* underneath your network.

If you entered the password incorrectly, you should instead see a message telling you that the network security key isn't correct. In that case, try typing the password again. Note that some establishments will load an internet page requiring you to accept their terms of use before you can connect.

It is possible for information you send over a public Wi-Fi connection to be intercepted by other people, so you should avoid using a public connection to access sensitives sites such as online banking.

SOLUTIONS

If an activity has stumped you, look no further—you're in the right place! These are the solutions to every activity in the book. If you're really stuck, review the section where the activity appears. If you find yourself flipping to the solutions frequently, don't lose heart—just keep practicing!

LESSON 1

Activity #1

1. Click the **start button**.
2. The popular apps tiles are displayed on the right side of the Start menu. The Weather app should look something like this:

3. The full apps list is shown on the left side of the Start menu. Scroll down until you find the Weather app.
4. Click the **start button** or anywhere else outside of the Start menu.

Activity #2

1. Click the **start button**. Click the **News** tile, or click in the search box, type **news**, and click **News**.
2. Follow the instructions on your screen to set up the app. Click an article to read it.
3. Click the **maximize button** in the top-right corner.
4. Click the **close button** in the top-right corner.

Lesson Review

1. Press the power button on your computer.
2. Enter the username and password you created in "Creating a Microsoft Account" on page 20.

3. Click the **start button**. Scroll through the list of apps in the Start menu, or click in the search box and type **calculator**.
4. Click the app to open it.
5. Press the calculator buttons by clicking them with your mouse.
6. Click the **close button** in the top-right corner.

LESSON 2

Activity #3

1. Click the **start button**. Click the **Microsoft Solitaire Collection** tile, or click in the search box, type **solitaire**, and click **Microsoft Solitaire Collection**.
2. Click the **Spider** button.
3. Read the guide if you're not sure how to play, and play through a game.
4. Click the **close button** in the top-right corner.

Activity #4

1. Click the **New event** button, fill out the event details, and click **Save and close**.
2. Click the **New event** button and fill out the event details. Click in the **Reminder** box and choose when you want to be reminded about the event. Click **Save and close**.
3. Click the **close button** in the top-right corner.

(continued)

Lesson Review

1. Use the Start menu to open the **Microsoft Solitaire Collection** app, click **FreeCell**, and then win a game!
2. Use the Start menu to open the **Weather** app. Find tomorrow's maximum temperature in the forecast.
3. Use the Start menu to open the **Calendar** app. Click the **New event** button. Under details, enter **Complete Lesson 3**, assign a date sometime next week, and adjust the time slots to allot at least two hours.
4. Click the **start button** and browse the Start menu for new apps to explore. When you find one you like, click the app to open it.

LESSON 3

Activity #5

1. Take photos of your garden or room.
2. Plug the cable that came with your camera into both the camera and your computer.
3. Open the **Photos** app, click **Import**, select the photos you want to import, and click **Continue**. Make sure the box labeled **Delete imported items from [your device] after importing** is unchecked, and then click the **Import** button.

Activity #6

1. Open the **Photos** app and click the **Collection** button at the top of the window. Click the collection of photos you took in Activity #5.
2. Click the photo you want to delete and then click the **delete button** at the top of the screen. Click **Delete** to confirm.

Lesson Review

1. Snap a few shots with your phone or camera.
2. Plug the cable that came with your camera into both the camera and your computer.
3. Open the **Photos** app, click **Import**, select the photos you want to import, and click **Continue**. Make sure the box labeled **Delete imported items from [your device] after importing** is unchecked, and then click the **Import** button.
4. Click the photo you want to edit. Click **Edit & Create** at the top of the screen. Click **Enhance your photo** and use the slider to improve your photo. Click the **Adjust** tab and use the sliders to further improve your photo. Finally, click **Save** and use the **back button** in the top-left corner to return to the list of photos.
5. Click the photo you want to delete. Click the **delete button** and then click **Delete** to confirm you want to delete the photo.
6. Click the photo you want to print. Click the **print button**. Ensure the printer settings are correct and then click the **Print** button.

LESSON 4

Activity #7

* If you see a blue line to the left of the email, you haven't read it before.
* The sender's name appears at the top of the email.
* The date the email was sent appears on the right.

Activity #8

1. Click **New mail**, and a new email box should appear on the right. Click in the **To** field and type the recipient's email address. Click in the **Subject** field and type a subject. Click in the box underneath the Subject and type your message. Click **Send**.
2. Wait until you receive a reply in your Inbox. Click it, and the message will open on the right. Read the message.
3. Click the **Reply** button at the top of the email. Type your message and click **Send**.

Activity #9

1. Click **New mail**, and a new email box should appear on the right. Click in the **To** field and type the recipient's email address. Click in the **Subject** field and type a subject. Click in the box underneath the Subject and type your message.
2. Click **Insert** and then click **Files**. Click the **Pictures** folder on the left side of the screen. Click the picture you want to send and then click **Open**.
3. Click **Send**.

Activity #10

1. Find an email in your Inbox that has a paper clip icon next to it (indicating an attachment).
2. Click the email and then click the attachment at the top of the message.
3. Click the **close button**.
4. Click the **Delete** button above the email.

Lesson Review

1. Use the Start menu to find and open the **Mail** app.
2. Click **New mail**, and a new email box should appear on the right. Click in the **To** field and type the recipient's email address. Click in the **Subject** field and type a subject.
3. Click in the box underneath the Subject and type your message, including a request that your friend send you a reply. Click **Send**.
4. Wait until you receive a reply in your Inbox. Click it, and the message will open on the right. Read the message.
5. Click **Reply** and type your message. Click **Insert** and then click **Files**. Click the **Pictures** folder on the left side of the screen. Click the picture you want to send and then click **Open**. Click **Send**.
6. Click your friend's email and then click **Delete**.

LESSON 5

Activity #11

The web address is *www.nostarch.com.*

Activity #12

1. Click in the address bar at the top of the screen. Type **www.washingtonpost.com** and press ENTER.
2. Click in the address bar. Type **www.nytimes.com** and press ENTER.
3. Click in the address bar. Type **www.nostarch.com** and press ENTER.

Activity #13

1. Click in the address bar. Type **www.nostarch.com** and press ENTER.
2. Click the title or cover for one of the books.

Activity #14

1. If you're not already at the No Starch website, click in the address bar. Type **www.nostarch.com** and press ENTER. Click the title or cover for one of the books on the No Starch site to visit that book's web page. Click the **back button** to return to the main No Starch page.
2. Click the **forward button** to return to the book's page.

Activity #15

1. Click the **more actions button** and click the **− button** until the zoom reads 75%.
2. Click the **more actions button** and click the **+ button** until the zoom reads 100%.

Activity #16

1. Click in the address bar, type **www.nostarch.com**, and press ENTER. Click the **add to favorites button** and then click **Add**.
2. Click in the address bar, type **www.washingtonpost.com**, and press ENTER. Click the **add to favorites button** and then click **Add**.
3. Click the **hub button**. Make sure you are looking at the list of favorites; if not, click the **star button** above the list. Click the **No Starch Press** favorite.
4. Click the **hub button**. Make sure you are looking at the list of favorites; if not, click the **star button** above the list. Right-click the **Washington Post** favorite and then click **Delete**.

Lesson Review

1. Open **Microsoft Edge** from the taskbar or the Start menu.
2. Click in the address bar, type **www.latimes.com**, and press ENTER.
3. Click an article in the list to read it.
4. Click the **more actions button** and click **Print**. Ensure that the printer settings are correct and then click **Print**.
5. Click the **back button**.
6. Click the **add to favorites button** and then click **Add**.
7. Click the **close button** in the top-right corner.
8. Open **Microsoft Edge** from the taskbar or the Start menu. Click the **hub button**. Make sure you are looking at the list of favorites; if not, click the **star button** above the list. Click the **Los Angeles Times** favorite.

LESSON 6

Activity #17

* Use the address bar to search for "biggest city in australia" and then click links until you find the answer, which is Sydney.

* Searching for something like "president before abraham lincoln" might work but is likely to produce mixed results. A more specific search, such as "list of united states presidents," will almost certainly give you better results. You should find that the answer is James Buchanan.

* Searches like "what to feed a rabbit," "rabbit food," and "healthy rabbit food" should all give you good results. Fresh hay, fruits, vegetables, and good-quality pellets are all good answers.

* A search like "foods reduce cholesterol" should produce good results. Oatmeal, fish, nuts, and avocados are all good answers.

Activity #18

1. Click in the address bar, type a search term, and press ENTER. Click the **Images** button.
2. Click the image you want to print to make it larger. Click the enlarged image to open it in a new tab.
3. Click the **more actions button** and click **Print**. Ensure that the printer settings are correct and then click **Print**.
4. Click the **close button** on the right side of the tab.
5. The **View page** button is located below the image, on the left side.

Lesson Review

1. Open **Microsoft Edge**. Click in the address bar, type **puppy housebreaking** or something similar, and press ENTER. Click one of the results to view the page and read it. Click the **back button** and then click another result to get a second opinion.

2. Click in the address bar, type **online safety tips** or something similar, and press ENTER. Click a page and read it. Click the **back button** and click another result to get a second opinion.

3. Click in the address bar, type **birthday cake** or something similar, and press ENTER. Click **Images**.

4. Click an image to enlarge it. Click the image again to open it in its own tab. Click the **more actions button** and click **Print**. Ensure that the printer settings are correct and then click **Print**. Click the **close button** on the right side of the tab to return to the list of images.

LESSON 7

Activity #19

1. Click one of the videos on the YouTube page.
2. Move your mouse over the video screen. Move the mouse to the volume control, and click and drag the slider left or right to achieve a suitable volume.
3. Click the **pause button**.

(continued)

4. Click the **play button**, which appears in place of the pause button.
5. Click the **full screen button**.
6. Click the **exit full screen button**, which appears in place of the full screen button.
7. Click a video from the "Up next" list on the right.
8. Click the **back button** twice.

Activity #20

1. Click in the YouTube search box, type a search term like **how to change a car tire**, and then press ENTER.
2. Click one of the results to watch it.

Lesson Review

1. Open **Microsoft Edge**. Click in the address bar, type **www.youtube.com**, and then press ENTER. Click a video.
2. Click the **back button**. Click in the YouTube search box, type the name of the movie you want to search for, and then press ENTER. Click a trailer in the list of results.

LESSON 8

Activity #21

1. Click **Apps** at the top of the screen, scroll to the bottom of the page to find the Categories section, and then click **Education**.
2. Click the **Chart** box and then click **Top free** from the list.

Activity #22

1. Click in the search box, type **microsoft jigsaw**, and press ENTER. Click **Microsoft Jigsaw** from the search results.
2. Click **Get**.
3. Click **Play**.

Lesson Review

1. Open the **Store** from the Start menu.
2. Click **Games** at the top of the screen and then scroll down to the list of categories. Click **Puzzle & trivia**, click **Microsoft Mahjong**, and then click **Get**.
3. Click **Play** to start the game. Close any pop-ups that appear. Click the **Choose puzzle** button and then click a difficulty and a puzzle. Click the **OK** button and either follow or skip the tutorial. Match tiles to win the game.
4. Close the game. Click the **start button** and then scroll down the list of apps to Microsoft Mahjong. Right-click **Microsoft Mahjong** and then click **Uninstall**. Click **Uninstall** again.

LESSON 9

Activity #23

1. Click the **Search** button, type **billy joel** into the search box, and then press ENTER. Click the **play button** next to one of the songs in the list that appears.

(continued)

2. Click the **Browse** button and click the **Genres & Moods** heading. Click **Jazz** and then click one of the playlists. Click the **Play** button.

Lesson Review

1. Open **Microsoft Edge**, type **play.spotify.com** into the address bar, and then press ENTER to go to the Spotify Play website. If you're asked to log in again, click **Already have an account? Log in here**. Type your email address and password, click the **I'm not a robot** box, and then click **Login**. Click the **Search** button, type the name of the artist you're looking for, and then press ENTER.
2. Click the **Browse** button and then click the **Genres & Moods** heading. Click a genre of music you like and then click a playlist. Click the **Play** button.

LESSON 10

Activity #24

1. Click the **Subjects** button and then click a genre you like. Click the cover picture of a book that looks interesting.
2. Click **Borrow** to borrow the book.
3. Click **Go to Loans** and then click **Download**.

Activity #25

1. Click the **back button** in the top left to return to your bookshelf. Click the book you downloaded in Activity #24.
2. Click in the middle of the screen and then click **Settings**. Click the **Font Size** box and choose a suitable font size.

3. Click the right edge of the book to flip to the next page.
4. Click in the middle of the screen and then click **More**. From the list that appears, click **Delete/Return**. Click **Delete and return** to confirm.

Lesson Review

1. Open **OverDrive** from the Start menu. Click your local library from the list on the right and then click **Search**. Type the name of the book you want and press ENTER.
2. Click the **Subjects** button and then click a genre you like. Click the cover picture of the book you want to borrow and then click **Borrow**. Click **Go to Loans** and then click **Download**.
3. Click the **back button** in the top left to return to your bookshelf, and click the book you just downloaded. Read the book by clicking the right side of the book to flip the pages. Click in the middle of the screen and then click **More**. From the list that appears, click **Delete/Return**. Click **Delete and return** to confirm.

LESSON 11

Activity #26

Click the **contacts button** and then click in the **Search Skype** box. Type the name, email address, or cell phone number of a friend into the search box. Click your friend from the list and then click **Add to Contacts**.

(continued)

Activity #27

1. Ask a friend to add you to Skype. You can give them your email address to make it easier for them to find you.
2. Click **Recent conversations** and then click your friend's name. Click **Accept** to confirm their contact request.

Activity #28

From your contacts list, click the friend you want to call, and then click the **video call button**.

Activity #29

1. From your contacts list, click the friend you want to send a message to. Click in the **Type a message** box and type your message. Press ENTER to send it.
2. When your friend replies, type a new message. Click the **emoticon button** and then click the emoticon you want to send. Press ENTER to send the message.

Lesson Review

1. Open **Skype** from the Start menu.
2. Click the **contacts button** and then click in the **Search Skype** box. Type the name, email address, or cell phone number of a friend into the search box. Click your friend from the list and then click **Add to Contacts**.
3. Click the **contacts button**, click the friend you want to call, and then click the **call button**.
4. From your contacts list, click the friend you want to call and then click the **video call button**.
5. When you receive the incoming call from your friend, click the **Audio** or **Video** button to answer the call.

6.   Click the **contacts button** and then click the friend you want to send a message to. Click in the **Type a message** box and type your message. Click the **emoticon button** and then click the emoticon you want to send. Press ENTER to send the message.

LESSON 12

Activity #30

* Home ribbon
* View ribbon
* File menu
* Home ribbon
* Quick Access Bar

Activity #31

1.   Click the page and use the keyboard to type the sentence.
2.   Press BACKSPACE twice to remove two exclamation marks.

Activity #32

1.   Click before the word *WordPad* and click and drag your mouse over it to highlight. Click the **underline button** on the Home ribbon.

(continued)

2. Click anywhere on the screen to deselect the word *WordPad*. Click before the first word in the sentence, and click and drag your mouse over the entire sentence to highlight. Click the arrow next to the Font Size box and click **16** from the list that appears.
3. Click the arrow next to the text color button and choose blue from the list that appears.

Activity #33

1. Click at the beginning of the first line, before the word *WordPad*, and press ENTER.
2. Click the line above the word *WordPad* and use the keyboard to type.
3. Click before the word *My*, and click and drag your mouse over the heading to highlight. Click the arrow next to the Font Size box and click **24** from the list that appears.
4. Click the **center align button** in the Home ribbon.
5. Click after the word *Document* to deselect the heading. Press ENTER and type the date.
6. Click the **right align button** in the Home ribbon. Your document should now look like this:

My First Document

October 10, 2017

WordPad is a great program!

Lesson Review

1. Open **WordPad** from the Start menu.
2. Use the keyboard to type a recipe.
3. Highlight words or sentences that you want to format by clicking and dragging your mouse over them and then using the formatting features in the Home ribbon.

4. Click **File** and then click **Save**. Make sure your document has a reasonable name such as *Vegetable Lasagna Recipe*. Click **Save**.
5. Click the **close button** in the top-right corner.
6. Open **WordPad** from the Start menu.
7. Use the keyboard to type a heading and a to-do list. Place your cursor in the heading and click the **center align button** in the Home ribbon.
8. Click **File** and then click **Save**. Make sure your document has a reasonable name such as *To-Do List*. Click **Save**.
9. Highlight your to-do list and click the **list button** in the Home ribbon (located above the right align button).
10. Click the **close button** in the top-right corner.

LESSON 13

Activity #34
1. Click **File Explorer** from the taskbar and then click **This PC** in the navigation pane.
2. Double-click the **Documents** folder.

Activity #35
1. Click **File Explorer** from the taskbar and then click the **Documents** folder in the navigation pane.
2. Click the **Home** ribbon and then click **New folder**. Type **Curry Recipes** as the name of the folder and then press ENTER.

(continued)

3. Click the *Curry Recipes* folder. Click the **Home** ribbon and then click **Rename**. Type **Lasagna Recipes** as the name of the folder and then press ENTER.
4. Click the *Lasagna Recipes* folder. Click the **Home** ribbon and then click **Delete**.
5. Close the **close button** in the top-right corner. Double-click the **Recycle Bin** icon on the desktop and then click the *Lasagna Recipes* folder. Click the **Manage** ribbon and then click **Restore the selected items**.

Activity #36

1. Open **WordPad** from the Start menu.
2. Type an apple cake recipe.
3. Click **File** and then click **Save**. Double-click the **Cake Recipes** folder. Click in the **File name** box, type **Apple Cake**, and then click **Save**.

Activity #37

1. Open **WordPad** from the Start menu.
2. Type a meat lasagna recipe.
3. Click **File** and then click **Save**. Click in the **File name** box, type **Meat Lasagna**, and then click **Save**. Click the **close button** in the top-right corner.
4. Click **File Explorer** from the taskbar and then click the **Documents** folder in the navigation pane.
5. Click the **Meat Lasagna** file. Click the **Home** ribbon and then click **Cut**. Double-click the **Lasagna Recipes** folder. Click the **Home** ribbon and then click **Paste**.

Activity #38

1. Click **File Explorer** from the taskbar and then click the **Documents** folder in the navigation pane.

2. Click the **Cake Recipes** folder. Click the **Home** ribbon and then click **Copy**. Click the **USB flash drive** folder in the navigation pane. Click the **Home** ribbon and then click **Paste**.

3. Click the **USB flash drive** folder in the navigation pane.

4. Double-click the **Cake Recipes** folder.

5. Click the **close button** in the top-right corner.

Lesson Review

1. Open **WordPad** from the Start menu. Type a soup recipe. Click **File** and then click **Save**. Type a name for your recipe and then click **Save**. Close the document.

2. Click **File Explorer** from the taskbar and then click the **Documents** folder in the navigation pane. Click the **Home** ribbon and then click **New folder**. Type **Soup Recipes** as the name of the folder and then press ENTER.

3. Click the recipe you just created. Click the **Home** ribbon and then click **Cut**. Double-click the **Soup Recipes** folder. Click the **Home** ribbon and then click **Paste**.

4. Click **View** and then click **Large icons**.

5. Open **WordPad** from the Start menu. Type a soup recipe. Click **File** and then click **Save**. Open the **Documents** folder and then open the **Soup Recipes** folder. Type a name for your recipe and click **Save**. Close the document.

6. Plug the USB flash drive into any spare USB port on your computer.

7. Click **File Explorer** from the taskbar and then click the **Documents** folder in the navigation pane. Click the **Soup Recipes** folder. Click the **Home** ribbon and then click **Copy**. Click the **USB flash drive** folder in the navigation pane. Click the **Home** ribbon and then click **Paste**.

LESSON 14

Lesson Review

1. Open **Microsoft Edge** and type **support.microsoft.com** into the address bar. Click in the search bar, type **how to organize apps**, and then click the first result.
2. Open the **Mail** app. Check your inbox for any scams or phishing emails. If an email looks suspicious, click it and then click **Delete**.

Index

Computers for Seniors is set in Avenir and Ziclets. The book was printed and bound by Versa Printing in East Peoria, Illinois. The paper is 60# Skyland Smooth. This book uses a layflat binding, in which the pages are bound together with a cold-set, flexible glue and the first and last pages of the resulting book block are attached to the cover. The cover is not actually glued to the book's spine, and when open, the book lies flat and the spine doesn't crack.